# COUNTRIES OF THE WORLD

# Vietnam

**Gareth Stevens Publishing**
A WORLD ALMANAC EDUCATION GROUP COMPANY

**About the Author:** Amy Condra-Peters is a freelance journalist currently living in Ho Chi Minh City. Her assignments and travels have taken her to many parts of Vietnam and enabled her to discover the amazing strength of the Vietnamese people.

## PICTURE CREDITS

Allsport/Stanley Chou: 36
ANA Press Agency/Jean Rey: 32 (top), 44
Michele Burgess: 29, 40 (both), 48, 61
Camera Press: 31, 49 (bottom), 80
Canadian Press: 83
Embassy of the Socialist Republic of
    Vietnam: 15 (bottom)
Ron Emmons: 34, 35
Alain Evrard: 3 (center), 5, 24, 45, 52, 91
Getty Images/HultonArchive: 15 (top),
    77, 78, 85
HBL Network Photo Agency: cover,
    3 (bottom), 7 (bottom), 46, 50,
    53 (bottom), 55, 72, 76, 81
Dave G. Houser: 32 (bottom), 69
The Hutchison Library: 1, 4, 6, 7 (top),
    11, 18, 19, 22, 25, 27 (bottom), 38,
    53 (top), 68
John R. Jones: 9 (top), 33, 37, 43, 51, 70
Björn Klingwall: 28
North Wind Picture Archive: 12
Christine Osborne: 3 (top), 30, 47, 89
Photobank Photolibrary: 9 (bottom), 10, 64,
    66, 67, 71, 82
Topham Picturepoint: 13, 14, 16, 39, 41, 58,
    74, 75, 79, 84
Travel Ink/Colin Marshall: 2, 59, 73
Trip Photographic Library: 17, 23, 49 (top),
    60, 62, 63
Marc Wang/Ng Lay San: 90 (both)
Alison Wright: 8, 20, 21, 26, 27 (top), 42,
    54, 56, 57
WWF/Mike Baltzer/Cat Tien National Park
    Conservation Project: 65

Digital Scanning by Superskill Graphics Pte Ltd

Written by
**AMY CONDRA-PETERS**

Edited by
**KAREN KWEK**

Edited in the U.S. by
**PATRICIA LANTIER**
**MONICA RAUSCH**

Designed by
**LYNN CHIN**

Picture research by
**SUSAN JANE MANUEL**

First published in North America in 2002 by
**Gareth Stevens Publishing**
A World Almanac Education Group Company
330 West Olive Street, Suite 100
Milwaukee, Wisconsin 53212 USA

Please visit our web site at
www.garethstevens.com
For a free color catalog describing
Gareth Stevens' list of high-quality books
and multimedia programs, call
1-800-542-2595 (USA) or
1-800-461-9120 (CANADA).
Gareth Stevens Publishing's
Fax: (414) 332-3567.

© **TIMES MEDIA PRIVATE LIMITED 2002**
Originated and designed by
Times Editions
An imprint of Times Media Private Limited
A member of the Times Publishing Group
Times Centre, 1 New Industrial Road
Singapore 536196
http://www.timesone.com.sg/te

**Library of Congress Cataloging-in-Publication Data**
Condra-Peters, Amy.
    Vietnam / by Amy Condra-Peters.
        p. cm. — (Countries of the world)
    Includes bibliographical references and index.
    Summary: An overview of the Socialist Republic of Vietnam, including
    information on its geography, history, government, social life and
    customs, and relationship with the United States.
    ISBN 0-8368-2348-6 (lib. bdg.)
    1. Vietnam—Juvenile literature. [1. Vietnam.] I. Title.
    II. Countries of the world (Milwaukee, Wis.)
        DS556.3.C68    2002
    959.704—dc21                    2001042986

Printed in Malaysia

1 2 3 4 5 6 7 8 9 06 05 04 03 02

# Contents

# AN OVERVIEW OF VIETNAM

Located in Southeast Asia, the Socialist Republic of Vietnam spans about 1,025 miles (1,650 kilometers) from northwest to southeast. This long, narrow country is home to more than fifty different ethnic groups.

Vietnam endured centuries of Chinese domination followed by French control, before declaring its independence in 1945. It was not until 1954, however, that communist-led northern Vietnamese forces defeated the French. From 1954 to 1976, Vietnam was divided into North Vietnam and South Vietnam. On July 2, 1976, the two halves were officially united as the Socialist Republic of Vietnam. After years of political isolation, Vietnam gradually opened its doors to the international community in the 1990s. For the Vietnamese people, the twenty-first century is a time of peace and promise.

*Opposite:* **Boys in Ho Chi Minh City have fun flying their kites.**

*Below:* **The people of Qui Nhon gather at a daily fish market by the sea. The fishing industry is a key part of the coastal economy in Vietnam.**

## THE FLAG OF VIETNAM

The flag of Vietnam bears a single yellow star on a solid red background. The star's five points stand for the farmers, workers, intellectuals, youth, and soldiers of Vietnam. The color red represents revolution and the Vietnamese struggle for independence. The flag was first officially presented to the Vietnamese people in 1945. After slight modifications made in 1955, the design was approved as the national flag.

5

# Geography

Covering an area of 127,243 square miles (329,560 square kilometers), Vietnam is shaped like an elongated letter *S*. The country borders China to the north, Laos and Cambodia to the west, the Gulf of Thailand to the southwest, the South China Sea to the southeast, and the Gulf of Tonkin to the northeast. The capital of Vietnam is Hanoi.

## Highlands

Mountains and hills cover about three-quarters of Vietnam's total land area. The rugged Fan Si Pan-Sa Phin range extends across the northwestern part of the country between the Red and Black rivers. The range includes Vietnam's highest peak, Mount Fan Si Pan at 10,312 feet (3,143 meters). The Annamese Cordillera extends parallel to the coast for about 700 miles (1,126 km) between the Red River Delta and the Central Highlands. This mountain range separates Vietnam from Laos.

**THE MEKONG RIVER**

**The Mekong River has always played a key part in Vietnam's geography, history, and economy. The river's delta is Vietnam's chief rice-growing region and a haven for wildlife.**
*(A Closer Look, page 69)*

*Below:* Forests, streams, and waterfalls characterize Vietnam's Central Highlands. Hill farms and coffee, tea, and rubber plantations stretch across the region's plateaus.

## Rivers and Deltas

Vietnam's two main rivers are the Red River in northern Vietnam and the Mekong River in the southern part of the country. The Red River flows through Vietnam from China's Yunnan Province and empties into the Gulf of Tonkin. The Mekong River, Southeast Asia's longest river, begins in north central China and crosses several other Asian countries before draining into the South China Sea near Ho Chi Minh City.

The Red River and Mekong deltas are Vietnam's most populated areas. Although the Vietnamese have built numerous dams, canals, and levees to control the Red River's flow, the Red River Delta remains vulnerable to severe flooding each year during the monsoon, or rainy summer season. Rice fields grown on the rich soils of the Mekong Delta produce almost half of Vietnam's total rice crop. This sprawling delta — almost four times as large as the Red River Delta — also supports sugarcane, banana, and coconut plantations.

## The Eastern Coastal Plain

Between the Red River and Mekong deltas lies a narrow coastal plain facing the South China Sea. Major seaports in this area include Da Nang, Nha Trang, and Vung Tau. The plain also supports coconut plantations and avocado and banana farms.

*Above:* Clear waters beckon off the coast of Nha Trang. The city is known for its port and its beautiful beaches.

**HA LONG BAY**

Steeped in mystery and legend, the islands and caves of Ha Long Bay, in the Gulf of Tonkin, offer many intriguing natural wonders.
*(A Closer Look, page 54)*

## The Northern Climate

In the northern parts of Vietnam, hot and rainy weather generally lasts from May to October. Heavy rainfalls and violent typhoons are frequent throughout these summer months. Summer temperatures in northern Vietnam average about 86° Fahrenheit (30° Celsius). During the dry winter season from November to April, temperatures and humidity levels drop dramatically. The north central coast experiences drizzle and mist in February and March. In the mountains, fine rain is accompanied by fog. Winter temperatures average 61° F (16° C).

## The Southern Climate

The south central lowlands and the Mekong Delta region have a year-round tropical climate with three seasons. November, December, and January generally bring the coolest temperatures of the year. The hot season lasts from about February to May, when temperatures can rise to about 96° F (35° C). The rainy season begins in May or June and lasts until October or November. Thunderstorms occur almost daily during this period.

*Above:* Women work in the rice fields of northern Vietnam. Rice is planted during the warm, humid months of summer in northern Vietnam and during the rainy season in southern Vietnam.

# Plants and Animals

The jungles, forests, swamps, and waterways of Vietnam are home to thousands of wildlife species, including some of Asia's rarest animals. In the nineteenth and twentieth centuries, zoologists in Vietnam discovered other rare species, such as the Vu Quang ox, the giant muntjac, and Edward's pheasant. Vietnam's forests also provide homes for Indian elephants, rhinoceroses, tigers, leopards, bears, snub-nosed monkeys, deer, wild cattle, and crocodiles. The waters off Vietnam's eastern coast contain seabed minerals and diverse marine life. Overfishing, however, threatens the wildlife in this region. The Vietnamese government and private organizations are considering plans to establish marine conservation programs.

Vietnam is home to more than ten thousand plant species, some of which have not yet been identified or named. Many of Vietnam's plants are valuable commercially as sources of food, medicine, or timber. Vietnam has abundant oak, beech, chestnut, pine, and teak forests. The country's other plants include needle trees, rhododendrons, and the rare dwarf bamboo.

*Above:* **Vietnam's many flowering plants include beautiful orchids.**

## THE JAVAN RHINOCEROS

The Javan rhinoceros, considered the world's rarest large mammal, lives in the steep hills of Vietnam's Central Highlands. (*A Closer Look, page 64*)

## ENDANGERED!

Many of Vietnam's animals, such as the Indian elephant (*left*), kouprey, tiger, and otter civet, are facing the possibility of extinction. Widespread hunting and poaching have decreased their numbers, and their natural habitats are disappearing as farmers and loggers clear away Vietnam's lush forests. The World Wide Fund for Nature is working with Vietnam's Ministry of Forestry to develop wildlife conservation programs in Vietnam.

# History

Most historians believe modern Vietnamese are descended from early rice-cultivating cultures, such as the Viet people and the Dong Son culture. The Viet lived in the Red River Delta and in parts of China during the first millennium B.C. Remains of the Dong Son culture, found in northern Vietnam, date back to 300 B.C. Southern Chinese forces repeatedly invaded the northern half of Vietnam and finally conquered the region in the second century B.C. The Chinese named this area Annam and controlled it until the tenth century A.D. Under Chinese rule, Vietnam was influenced by elements of Chinese culture and civilization, including Confucianism and ancestor worship; methods of rice cultivation and flood control; and achievements in the arts and sciences. China also forced the Vietnamese people to pay high taxes and submit to foreign rule.

After numerous unsuccessful uprisings, northern Vietnam broke free from Chinese rule in 939 to become an independent kingdom ruled by Vietnamese dynasties. Despite freedom from China, however, heavy taxation continued throughout northern Vietnam, and the new state endured peasant uprisings, Mongol invasions, and political unrest.

**THE KINGDOM OF CHAMPA**

While dynasties reigned in northern Vietnam, the ancient Islamic state of Champa ruled the central coast. Established in the second century A.D. by a Malay-Polynesian people called the Cham, Champa had an Indian-influenced culture different from that of the Chinese-influenced northern Vietnamese. From the tenth century to its collapse in the seventeenth century, the kingdom of Champa frequently engaged in battle with both the northern Viet people and the Cambodian Khmer empire that ruled the Mekong Delta region.

*Left:* **Chinese influence is apparent in the architecture of the Pavilion of Splendor, part of the imperial complex at the Nguyen Dynasty's capital in Hue.**

*Left:* **The tomb of Emperor Khai Dinh (r. 1916–1925) of the Nguyen Dynasty is located near the Perfume River a few miles (km) from Hue. During Emperor Khai Dinh's rule, Vietnam absorbed Western, especially French, influence.**

## The Le Dynasty

China reestablished control of northern Vietnam in 1407. By 1428, however, wealthy landowner Le Loi had led northern Vietnamese forces to victory against the Chinese army. Le Loi became Emperor Le Thai To, founder of the great Later Le Dynasty. Art, literature, and commerce flourished during this period. Under the Le emperors, northern Vietnam eventually defeated the kingdom of Champa in central Vietnam in the fifteenth century and won the Mekong Delta region from the Khmer empire in the mid-eighteenth century. Vietnam, however, remained divided. In theory, the Le Dynasty controlled all of Vietnam, but in practice, two powerful families established separate governments in Vietnam. The Trinh family dominated the northern part, and the Nguyen family controlled the central and southern parts.

## The Nguyen Dynasty

In the 1770s, the Tay Son family rebelled against both the Trinh and Nguyen families and controlled all of Vietnam for a brief period. By 1802, however, with French military assistance, a member of the Nguyen family had defeated the Tay Sons. He declared himself emperor, under the name Gia Long, and ruled all of Vietnam under one administration and one set of laws. The new dynasty, the Nguyen Dynasty, set up its capital in Hue.

**HUE: AN ANCIENT CAPITAL**

Hue was built on the banks of the Perfume River in central Vietnam in 1687. Many people consider this beautiful city the cultural, religious, and academic heart of Vietnam.

*(A Closer Look, page 62)*

**WESTERN POWERS IN VIETNAM**

The Portuguese and other European powers began arriving in Vietnam in the sixteenth century. In the late eighteenth and early nineteenth centuries, the French established significant relations with Vietnamese rulers by helping the Nguyen family defeat the Tay Son rebels.

## French Colonial Rule

Emperor Gia Long allowed French merchants and Catholic missionaries to live and work in Vietnam, but his successor, Minh Mang, began persecuting French and Vietnamese Catholics in the 1830s. France retaliated by attacking and capturing Saigon (now Ho Chi Minh City) in 1859. In 1862, Nguyen emperor Tu Duc signed a treaty that granted other southern provinces to France. The regions under French rule were combined to form the colony of Cochinchina. The French gradually extended their rule over all of Vietnam. By 1893, they controlled Cochinchina and four French protectorates — northern Vietnam (Tonkin), central Vietnam (Annam), Cambodia, and Laos.

French development projects, such as industries and transportation networks, were funded by taxes imposed on Vietnam's rural population. Debt often forced farmers to give up their land and become tenants for rich landowners. By the 1940s, about half of Vietnam's population had become landless. Taxation, the use of forced labor, and the seizure of private lands for mines and other industrial uses led to deep resentment of and growing resistance to French rule.

*Above:* **French troops captured the town of Lang Son, in northern Vietnam, in 1885. In name, the Nguyen emperors still ruled Vietnam. In practice, however, the French controlled the country by the late 1880s.**

## Nationalism and the Viet Minh

Japan invaded Vietnam during World War II (1939–1945). In 1941, nationalist leader Ho Chi Minh, who had been living overseas since 1911, returned to Vietnam. He and his followers organized a fiercely nationalistic communist resistance movement called the Viet Minh. With Vietnam in chaos after the surrender of the Japanese in 1945, the Viet Minh assumed complete control of northern and north central Vietnam (North Vietnam). Ho Chi Minh declared Vietnam's independence. The French, however, seized control of parts of southern Vietnam.

## The Indochina Wars

The First Indochina War broke out in late 1946, when the French insisted on reestablishing control over all of Vietnam. In 1954, the Viet Minh defeated the French at Dien Bien Phu, reaffirming the freedom of North Vietnam. French troops then withdrew from Vietnam.

Ngo Dinh Diem, a Roman Catholic who had served in the Nguyen royal court, made himself president of the Republic of Vietnam (South Vietnam) in 1955. In 1963, the Viet Cong — a southern, communist-led movement supported by North Vietnam — overthrew the Diem government, starting the Second Indochina War (also called the Vietnam War). The war ended on April 30, 1975, when communist forces entered the southern capital of Saigon. In 1976, North and South Vietnam were united as the Socialist Republic of Vietnam, with its capital at Hanoi.

**THE UNITED STATES AND THE VIETNAM WAR**

U.S. military advisers had been stationed in Vietnam in increasing numbers since 1955. After the overthrow of the Diem government in 1963, the U.S. government became alarmed at the threat of a communist victory in Vietnam. U.S. president Lyndon B. Johnson ordered the bombing of North Vietnam in 1965. Later that year, U.S. troops started arriving in South Vietnam. The United States withdrew from Vietnam in 1973, but the war between North and South Vietnam continued until 1975.

**THE CU CHI TUNNELS**

Part of a vast network of secret tunnels used by the Viet Cong during the Vietnam War, the Cu Chi Tunnels now attract tourists eager to explore the underground chambers and passages.
(*A Closer Look, page 48*)

*Left:* South Vietnamese president Ngo Dinh Diem (*back row, second from left*) poses here with family members in 1963. He was killed in the revolt that overthrew him later that year.

# The Socialist Republic of Vietnam

After the war, the reunified Vietnam began reconstructing its economy. Roads, bridges, schools, hospitals, and other structures damaged by bombing and gunfire also had to be rebuilt. The new communist regime saw many South Vietnamese journalists, intellectuals, and military and religious leaders as political threats and imprisoned them. Hundreds of thousands of Vietnamese fled the country for other Asian countries, Europe, and North America.

In 1978, border conflicts with Cambodia (Kampuchea) prompted Vietnamese troops to invade the country. Vietnamese forces overthrew the Cambodian Khmer Rouge government and installed a pro-Vietnamese government in the Cambodian capital of Phnom Penh. China, which supported the Khmer Rouge, briefly sent its troops to Vietnam in 1979. Vietnam's invasion of Cambodia also angered the international community. The United States and most other Western countries refused to trade with Vietnam.

In the late 1980s, Vietnam withdrew its forces from Cambodia, and most Western countries renewed diplomatic and commercial ties with the Vietnamese government. The Socialist Republic of Vietnam has emerged from its postwar isolation and is now gaining a stronger presence in the international community.

*Below:* **Vietnamese troops withdrew from Cambodia in 1989.**

## The Trung Sisters (?–A.D. 43)

From 200 B.C. until A.D. 939, Chinese forces repeatedly invaded what is now Vietnam and demanded high tax payments. The Vietnamese people deeply resented this foreign control. Two Vietnamese sisters, Trung Trac and Trung Nhi, vowed revenge. Mounted on elephants, the Trung sisters led thousands of fellow Vietnamese against Chinese forces in A.D. 40. The revolt drove the Chinese out of the country for a time, and the Trung sisters became queens of a newly freed state extending from southern China to what is now Hue. In A.D. 43, however, the Chinese returned to conquer Vietnam. Vietnamese legend has it that, rather than surrender to Chinese rule, the sisters drowned themselves in a river. Today, they are still honored throughout Vietnam as national warriors.

## Ho Chi Minh (1890–1969)

Born Nguyen Sinh Cung, Ho Chi Minh came from a poor family. He left Vietnam in 1911. From 1917 to the 1920s, he became involved with communist activities first in France, then in Russia and China. In 1930, he founded the Indochinese Communist Party (later renamed the Communist Party of Vietnam). He began to use the name *Ho Chi Minh* ("He Who Enlightens") in the 1940s. Returning to Vietnam in 1941, he led victorious Vietnamese forces against Japanese and French troops in northern and north central Vietnam. He served as president of the Democratic Republic of Vietnam (North Vietnam) from 1945 until his death in 1969.

**Ho Chi Minh**

## Nguyen Thi Binh (1927– )

Nguyen Thi Binh is one of Vietnam's most distinguished leaders. Born in the province of Quang Nam, she worked as a teacher after finishing secondary school. From 1951 to 1953, she was imprisoned for her involvement in anti-French political activity. In 1969, she became minister of foreign affairs in South Vietnam. Throughout the 1970s and 1980s, she held a variety of political offices and chair positions in international organizations. She was elected vice president of Vietnam in 1992 and reelected to the same position in 1997.

**Nguyen Thi Binh**

# Government and the Economy

The Socialist Republic of Vietnam is a one-party state ruled by the Communist Party of Vietnam. The powerful fifteen-member Political Bureau, or Politburo, headed by the General Secretary of the party, decides government policy. A national congress meets every five years to set the direction of the party. The Ninth Party Congress convened in 2001.

## System of Government

The National Assembly is the highest representative body of the people. Consisting of 450 elected members who serve for five-year terms, the National Assembly elects the president, vice

TOÀN ĐẢNG
TOÀN QUÂN
TOÀN DÂN

KIÊN ĐỊNH ĐI THEO CON ĐƯỜNG CỦA ĐẢNG VÀ BÁC HỒ ĐÃ CHỌN

*Left:* Images of the founder of the Communist Party of Vietnam, Ho Chi Minh, are displayed on banners, posters, and billboards all over Vietnam.

president, prime minister, and other key officials such as the leaders of the assembly.

As chief of state, the Vietnamese president nominates candidates for a number of key positions, including the Chief Justice of the Supreme People's Court, the country's highest court of appeal. The prime minister heads the government and oversees a cabinet that includes four deputy prime ministers and the heads of ministries and commissions.

The judicial branch of government is made up of a system of courts and the Supreme People's Procuracy. Overseen by the Supreme People's Court, the People's Courts and Military Tribunals operate at local and military levels, respectively. The Supreme People's Procuracy ensures that the government and all military, social, and economic organizations obey the law.

## Administration

Vietnam is divided into fifty-seven provinces and four municipalities. The provinces are further divided into smaller administrative units, each of which elects a local People's Council that handles executive matters. Voting in National Assembly and People's Council elections is compulsory for all Vietnamese citizens aged eighteen and above. Nominated candidates cannot stand for election without the approval of the Communist Party of Vietnam.

### HO CHI MINH

Ho Chi Minh was president of the Democratic Republic of Vietnam (North Vietnam) from 1945 until his death in 1969. In his determined fight for a united Vietnam free of foreign rule, he led forces against foreign armies. Today, he is widely regarded as the father of Vietnam.
*(A Closer Look, page 58)*

### HO CHI MINH CITY

Once the seat of the government of South Vietnam, Ho Chi Minh City is still known to some by its old name, Saigon. Today, the charms of its colonial heritage combine with increasing business opportunities to make Ho Chi Minh City Vietnam's primary economic and industrial center.
*(A Closer Look, page 60)*

## Economic Changes

After the Vietnam War, Vietnam was politically isolated, and its economy was slow to develop. The government launched a program of large-scale economic reform in 1986, marking a shift toward a more market-oriented economy. This change gave farmers the opportunity to decide for themselves which crops to grow and how to sell what they produced. Limited privatization was allowed, and small family-run businesses were established.

The reforms turned Vietnam into one of the fastest-growing economies in the world by the early 1990s. The quality of life for many Vietnamese people improved as average yearly incomes rose from about U.S. $220 in 1994 to about U.S. $372 by 1999. In 1994, the United States lifted the trade embargo it had imposed on Vietnam after the Vietnam War. The two countries signed a bilateral trade agreement in 2000. The agreement opens new markets for Vietnam's agricultural and industrial exports and increases U.S. investment in Vietnam. Although the Vietnamese government still controls most industries as well as the banking and foreign trade sectors, economic reform continues. In 2000, Vietnam opened its stock exchange, further signaling the country's willingness to explore a market-driven economy.

*Above:* **The Vietnamese government is investing increasingly in long-term economic projects, such as this hydroelectric dam project near Da Lat, in the Central Highlands.**

# Continued Economic Growth

While economic reform has stimulated industry and commerce throughout Vietnam, rural life remains difficult. Many people face seasonal unemployment, finding work only during harvest times. Other challenges to prosperity include a poor infrastructure and widespread government corruption. Nevertheless, an educated workforce and a continued commitment to economic reform promise future economic improvement for Vietnam.

Today, Vietnam's exports include rice, tea, coffee, rubber, textiles, garments, crude oil, footwear, marine products, and handicrafts. Vietnam's main trading partners are Japan, China, South Korea, Singapore, Taiwan, and France.

Wet-rice cultivation is Vietnam's main agricultural activity. Due to the success of recent agricultural reforms, Vietnam has become the world's second-largest exporter of rice after Thailand and the third-largest exporter of coffee after Brazil and Colombia. Other important cash crops include corn, sweet potatoes, peanuts, soybeans, rubber, cotton, tea, and cashew nuts. Tourism also is becoming an increasingly important industry. In 2000, about two million foreign tourists visited Vietnam.

**GETTING AROUND IN VIETNAM**

Visitors might find that traveling in Vietnam is sometimes difficult, with the country's crowded buses and slow trains. Other modes of transportation, however, such as passenger boats and *cyclos* (see-klohs), offer charming and scenic ways to travel.
*(A Closer Look, page 52)*

*Below:* Imports and exports make their way through the container terminals of busy ports such as Haiphong.

# People and Lifestyle

With a population of more than 78 million, Vietnam is one of the most densely populated countries in the world. Between 85 and 90 percent of Vietnam's population is ethnic Vietnamese, believed to be the descendants of early rice-cultivating peoples, such as the Viet. The Viet people originally occupied southern China and northern Vietnam thousands of years ago.

## Ethnic Minorities

Ethnic Vietnamese share their country with members of more than fifty minority ethnic groups. Hill groups, including the Tay, Tai, Muong, Nung, Hmong, and Giarai peoples, live in the mountains around the Red River Delta and in the Central Highlands. These hill groups form about 10 percent of Vietnam's population. Some of these groups have as few as one hundred members, while other groups number over a million. Most of these groups practice an agricultural, sometimes seminomadic, lifestyle. Other minorities in Vietnam include the Khmer, who are of Cambodian descent and live near the Cambodian border, and the Cham, who are

**THE DRAGON KING AND THE MOUNTAIN FAIRY**

Vietnamese folklore claims that the one hundred honored ancestors of all ethnic Vietnamese came from the union of a dragon king and a mountain fairy.
*(A Closer Look, page 50)*

*Left:* **A Vietnamese father spends time with his baby daughter in Hanoi.**

**URBAN AND RURAL DIFFERENCES**

Economic reforms have raised the standard of living for the Vietnamese, especially the citizens of Hanoi and Ho Chi Minh City. Many people who farm the remote countryside, however, live in extreme poverty. Many households in rural Vietnam do not have access to safe drinking water or sanitary facilities, such as toilets or running water.

descendants of the kingdom of Champa that once ruled Vietnam's central coast.

Many of the two million ethnic Chinese (Hoa) living in Vietnam are settled in southern Vietnam, where they have long been active in banking, trading, and commerce. Vietnamese of Chinese ancestry were persecuted after the country's reunification in 1975, and many ethnic Chinese left Vietnam as refugees. Today, however, ethnic Chinese businesspeople play a significant role in Vietnam's growing economy.

## Being Vietnamese

The Vietnamese are gracious people. Chinese Confucian traditions have influenced many Vietnamese customs, including the subordination of subject to ruler, son to father, wife to husband, and the young to their elders. For the Vietnamese, self-restraint is key to promoting social harmony. Public displays of emotion, such as shouting, arguing, or gesturing wildly, are frowned upon in a culture that values the virtues of dignity and politeness.

**THE HILL GROUPS OF VIETNAM**

The hill peoples of the northern and central highlands include the Hmong (*above*) and Muong groups.
*(A Closer Look, page 57)*

## The Importance of Family

Vietnamese life revolves around the family. Grandparents, parents, aunts, uncles, and children often live together in one house. The family structure in Vietnam is hierarchical. Children are expected to obey and honor their parents at all times, and younger children are taught to respect their older brothers and sisters. The Vietnamese consider the elderly, who have gained a lifetime of experience, the wisest and most respected members of society. Family members have an obligation to care financially for their relatives. Every working member of the family is expected to contribute part of his or her income to help shoulder the household expenses.

*Below:* **Many families rely on motorcycles and bicycles for transportation in Vietnam. Young children often ride with their parents.**

Family bonds extend even beyond the grave. Each year, on the anniversary of the death of a close ancestor, family members make formal offerings to please the spirit of the departed relative. This practice, known as ancestor worship, is based on the belief that the spirits of the dead continue to influence the living. The rituals of ancestor worship remind family members of their common bond and their dependence on each other.

## Vietnamese Women

Although Vietnamese culture emphasizes the submissive roles of women as daughters and wives, women exercise a great deal of

**GETTING MARRIED**

When a woman marries, she usually moves into the home of her husband's family. A bride's role as a daughter-in-law in her new family is almost as important as her status as wife.

22

influence in the family, especially concerning financial matters. Vietnamese women have always worked, whether in rice fields, factories, or offices. They are also expected to perform most household duties.

After reunification, Vietnam granted legal equality to women and men in most matters. Women, however, still found themselves in low-paying jobs, such as farm labor and rice planting. The Vietnamese Women's Union was founded in the 1930s and had about eight million members in 2000. The union has created a credit program designed to help rural women. Under the program, women can apply for small loans to set up or run their own businesses.

**THE AO DAI: A GRACEFUL OUTFIT**

Consisting of a long tunic worn over a pair of trousers, the traditional dress of Vietnamese women is both stylish and practical.
*(A Closer Look, page 45)*

In recent years, Vietnamese women have strengthened their influence in society. A growing number of capable women now occupy high public positions. Politician Nguyen Thi Binh has served as Vietnam's vice president since 1992.

*Above:* **A newly wed Vietnamese couple in Ho Chi Minh City poses for photographs.**

## Children's Roles

The Vietnamese people love children. Parents look to their children to care for them as they grow old and become unable to work. All children are expected to contribute to the family by helping with housework and caring for younger brothers and sisters or by working after school in a family business.

# Primary and Secondary Education

Vietnamese society places a high value on education. The Vietnamese government has been highly successful in promoting literacy and basic education. According to government figures, more than 90 percent of Vietnam's population can read and write, and all Vietnamese children attend primary schools.

Children usually begin school at the age of five or six, although nursery schools accept children aged three months to three years, and some children attend kindergarten from the age of three. Primary education in Vietnam lasts five years. Lower secondary school lasts four years, after which some students go on to attend upper, or specialized, secondary school for three years. Most schools are run in two sessions — morning and afternoon — in order to accommodate two groups of students. Schools are closed for the summer holidays, which last from June to September.

Despite its achievements, the Vietnamese educational system faces many challenges. Educational facilities in rural areas are frequently inadequate and may consist of little more than simple,

*Below:* **Primary school students in Ho Chi Minh City gather in the street after school.**

one-room schoolhouses. Schools also face a general shortage of teachers. Although school fees are low, many rural families cannot afford to give their children a complete education. Many children stop attending after primary school to help their family members work in the fields or markets.

*Above:* **Upper secondary students in Hanoi rejoice on their graduation day. A few students will go on to enroll at universities.**

## Higher Education

The Vietnamese government continues to stress the importance of education. Only by developing a workforce that is trained in telecommunications, biotechnology, and computer science will Vietnam be able to compete in a global economy.

A university education in Vietnam generally lasts four years. Today, about 500,000 students pursue higher studies in Vietnam. The country's most prestigious university, the National University of Hanoi, was founded in 1907. Other major universities are located in Hanoi, Hue, Ho Chi Minh City, and Da Nang. Students from universities and colleges worldwide, including institutions in the United States and Canada, have participated in exchange programs that allow them to study at Vietnam's universities.

### AN ANCIENT UNIVERSITY

**The first national university in Vietnam was founded in 1076 at the Temple of Literature in Hanoi. From the eleventh to the eighteenth centuries, the university trained young men in literature and philosophy. Today, the Temple of Literature still stands as a historical monument, but it no longer functions as a university.**

# Many Different Belief Systems

From 1976 to the mid-1980s, the communist government severely repressed religious activity. Since the mid-1980s, however, restrictions on religion have eased, and temples and churches have reopened throughout Vietnam. The government now recognizes six official religions: Buddhism, Roman Catholicism, Protestantism, Islam, and the Cao Dai and Hoa Hao faiths.

## Buddhism

Most Vietnamese people practice Buddhism, which was introduced in Vietnam in the second century A.D. Buddhism is founded on the teachings of Siddhartha Gautama, an Indian prince who lived in Nepal in the sixth century B.C. Buddhists believe that life is a continuous cycle of birth, death, and rebirth and that a person's actions in the present determine the quality of his or her next life.

## Christianity

Roman Catholic missionaries came to Vietnam from Europe in the sixteenth century. Under French rule, Roman Catholicism became a major religion in Vietnam. During the mid-1950s, when the

## OTHER BELIEFS

Confucianism is a code of ethics drawn up by Chinese philosopher Confucius in the sixth century B.C. Confucian teachings emphasize respect for authority, hierarchy, and a sense of duty to family and community. Taoism originated in China at about the same time as Confucianism. Taoist beliefs stress virtue, non-violence, harmony, and humility. Animism is the belief that spirits live in all things, including rocks, streams, and forests. Believers offer gifts of food, flowers, and incense to keep these spirits happy.

communist government was gaining power in North Vietnam, large numbers of Catholics fled south to avoid persecution. Most of Vietnam's eight million Catholics still live in the southern regions of the country. Outside of the Philippines, they represent the largest population of Catholics in Southeast Asia.

North American missionaries brought Protestantism to Vietnam in the nineteenth and twentieth centuries. Vietnamese Protestants number less than 250,000 today and are concentrated among the hill groups of the Central Highlands.

## The Hoa Hao Movement and Islam

The Hoa Hao faith was founded in Vietnam's Mekong Delta region in the twentieth century. Hoa Hao is a type of reformed Buddhism that favors simple worship over elaborate ceremonies. There are an estimated 2–3 million Hoa Hao followers in Vietnam.

Arab traders brought Islam to Vietnam in the seventh century. Today, Vietnam's Islamic population numbers about fifty thousand and lives mainly in south central Vietnam, the Mekong Delta, and close to the border with Cambodia.

**THE CAO DAI MOVEMENT**

Cao Dai combines elements of Buddhist, Confucian, Taoist, Christian, and Islamic beliefs. A giant, all-seeing Divine Eye (*above*) symbolizes the Supreme Spirit, or God.

*(A Closer Look, page 46)*

# Language and Literature

## The Vietnamese Language

Vietnamese is the most widely spoken language in Vietnam. Modern Vietnamese belongs to the Viet-Muong branch in the Austro-Asiatic group of languages. Viet-Muong languages, which are spoken in parts of Vietnam, Laos, and Cambodia, share a monosyllabic structure and a complex tonal system.

The first written form of Vietnamese appeared between the ninth and eleventh centuries. This script evolved from Chinese characters and was used in official, historical, and literary texts. In the thirteenth century, Vietnamese nationalists devised a new written language based on the Vietnamese pronunciation of Chinese characters. This script, *chu nom* (choo nahm), was commonly used in popular literature. In the seventeenth century, a French Jesuit scholar named Alexandre de Rhodes created another system of writing Vietnamese, using the Latin alphabet. In 1651, the first Romanized dictionary using this new script was published. Educated people initially looked down on the script, but it gained popularity because it was easier to learn than the older scripts. It has been the official version of Vietnamese since the 1920s. In addition to Vietnamese, the people of Vietnam also speak English, French, Chinese, Khmer, or their own ethnic languages.

Vietnamese is a tonal language, which means that the same words spoken in different tones have different meanings. The Vietnamese language has six tones. Speakers in different regions of the country often pronounce the same words with regional variations.

*Left:* The six tones of Vietnamese words are indicated by symbols above the words.

## Literature

Vietnam has a rich literary tradition. In the past, storytellers traveled from village to village, reciting satirical poems, legends, and fables explaining human nature. The first forms of written narrative in Vietnam appeared in about the tenth century. These early works often reflected classical Chinese plots and forms.

The eighteenth and nineteenth centuries were a time of great literary achievement in Vietnam. During this period, the poet Ho Xuan Huong wrote tales calling for equality for women. Celebrated poet Doan Thi Diem translated the Chinese poem *The Lament of a Warrior's Wife*, which became a well-known folk song.

During the 1930s, French authors inspired the Vietnamese to write prose as well as poetry. Later, nationalistic writings were popular during times of conflict with other countries. Modern writers often choose to write about personal relationships and daily life instead of politics. The communist government controls what is published in Vietnam and can censor works that are critical of the current regime.

*Above:* **A newsstand sells magazines in Ho Chi Minh City. The Vietnamese are avid readers.**

### A CLASSIC

In the late eighteenth century, Nguyen Du, a scholarly court official who served as an ambassador to China, wrote an epic poem describing the doomed love shared by a poet and the princess of the moon. This classic work, titled *Kim Van Kieu* (*The Tale of Kieu*), has become one of the most famous stories in Vietnam.

# Arts

For centuries, Chinese traditions have influenced the art and architecture of Vietnam. Vietnamese artists often decorate their paintings and carvings with fanciful images of dragons, tortoises, tigers, unicorns, or the fabled phoenix. These animals symbolize important virtues such as wisdom and perseverance.

## Early Vietnamese Art

Ancient bronze art found in northern Vietnam dates from about 300 B.C. The Dong Son, a seafaring people, created magnificent Chinese-style bronze drums carved with intricate geometric designs and scenes of village life. Bronze remained a popular sculptors' medium for centuries. Bronze statues of deities and mythical creatures, such as dragons and unicorns, decorate temples and pagodas throughout Vietnam.

During the tenth and eleventh centuries A.D., artists from the Indian-influenced kingdom of Champa carved beautiful figures from sandstone. Cham sculpture and architecture was renowned for its graceful lines.

*Below:* **The Cham built ornately decorated Hindu towers. Many of these beautiful structures still stand along Vietnam's central coastline.**

# Painting

Vietnamese artists traditionally painted only on silk stretched across wooden frames. Their paintings included rural landscapes and portraits of ancestors. In 1925, the French founded the École des Beaux-Arts de l'Indochine (later renamed the Hanoi College of Fine Arts) in Hanoi. Teachers taught Vietnamese artists the impressionist, realist, and symbolist techniques popular in Europe. Among the great Vietnamese painters to emerge from the school are Nguyen Sang, Nguyen Tu Nghiem, and Bui Xuan Phai, who combined Western and Asian techniques and inspired future generations of Vietnamese artists.

Contemporary Vietnamese artists are experimenting with new techniques and themes. Art schools and galleries have sprung up in Hanoi, Hue, and Ho Chi Minh City. Contemporary Vietnamese art has gained a following throughout the world, and exhibitions have been held in major international cities, such as New York, London, and Paris.

*Above: The Mekong River* **was painted by Vietnamese artist Hoang Lan Anh in 1993.**

**LACQUER AND LACQUERWARE**

**Usually clear but sometimes colored, lacquer is a substance applied to smooth surfaces in layers. Vietnamese lacquerware products are renowned for their elegance and durability.**
*(A Closer Look, page 66)*

*Left:* **A craftsman polishes the surface of a piece of furniture inlaid with mother-of-pearl.**

# Traditional Crafts

Vietnam is known for its mother-of-pearl inlay, embroidery, and pottery. The art of mother-of-pearl inlay has been practiced in Vietnam for one thousand years. This inlay technique involves carving designs into wooden objects, then inserting mother-of-pearl so that the white mollusk shells glow within the dark wood. Mother-of-pearl inlay is used to decorate furniture, cabinets, chests, and screens. One of the most famous pearl inlayers in Vietnam was Truong Cong Khanh. A general during the Ly Dynasty (1009–1225), Khanh is now known as the patron saint of craftspeople.

Embroidery is a craft widely practiced throughout Vietnam. Detailed designs of dragons, butterflies, and Chinese characters are embroidered onto silk and velvet to make cushion covers, table mats, and items of clothing.

Pottery has long been a significant traditional art form in Vietnam. Over centuries, each Vietnamese dynasty produced distinctive pottery colors and designs. Glazed animal figures, such as horses, cranes, and tortoises, were popular during the fifteenth century, and they are still being copied today.

## WATER PUPPETRY

**Snakes slither across cloudy ponds, dragons whirl around in circles, and monkeys shimmy to the top of coconut trees — such animated scenes make up the playful amusement of a water puppet show.**

*(A Closer Look, page 72)*

# Traditional Music

Traditional Vietnamese music is written not on the eight-note scale used in the West but primarily on a five-note scale of Chinese origin. It is played on traditional instruments such as the bamboo flute, the single-stringed lute, the bamboo xylophone, and a variety of drums and gongs.

# Opera

Vietnam has several types of traditional theater, or opera. *Cheo* (chay-oh) operas are the oldest form of theater in Vietnam. These performances combine dance, song, mime, and poetry. Rural people once performed these operas as a form of protest against wealthy landlords and French rulers.

*Tuong* (toong) performances are classical forms of opera that arrived in Vietnam from China in the fourteenth century. Actors wear elaborate costumes and makeup and act in exaggerated, stylized ways to perform these dramas. Tuong operas were staged in the royal courts of Vietnam's emperors and usually feature stories of legendary heroes.

*Cai luong* (kye loong) opera was introduced in Vietnam in 1920 and is popular in Vietnam's larger towns and cities. Cai luong performances use intricate backdrops and scenery and are based on more modern, realistic plots than the country's other operatic forms.

## CONTEMPORARY MUSIC

During the nineteenth and twentieth centuries, as court music declined, distinct northern and southern musical styles developed in Vietnam. Western classical music and styles of composition also grew in popularity. By the end of the twentieth century, traditional Vietnamese music had declined in popularity. Today, Western pop music and the music of Vietnamese singers who live overseas are extremely popular among the young people of Vietnam.

*Left:* The Nghia Binh Classical Opera Society performs tuong opera in the province of Binh Dinh.

# Leisure and Festivals

Urban Vietnamese enjoy visiting the parks in their towns and cities. In their leisure hours, many Vietnamese men gather in cafés or at sidewalk stalls to talk and play games such as chess, Chinese checkers, and cards. Because Vietnamese women are responsible for housework in addition to their paid jobs, they usually do not have as much leisure time as Vietnamese men do.

## Indoor Entertainment

The Vietnamese people are avid moviegoers. Vietnamese cinemas often show Western films dubbed or subtitled in Vietnamese. Vietnam also produces its own films; kung fu movies are especially popular. The Vietnamese also enjoy karaoke. A Japanese invention that has taken the world by storm, karaoke allows people to sing their favorite songs to the accompaniment of instrumental music, while the song lyrics are displayed on a video screen.

*Opposite:* **Lenin Park in Hanoi is a favorite spot for budding young painters.**

*Below:* **In the evenings and on weekends, couples and groups of friends meet to chat or stroll in Vietnam's shady parks. Parents take their young children to run and play in the parks. Children also enjoy the small toys, balloons, and cotton candy sold by park vendors.**

## Activities for Children

Many Vietnamese children belong to organizations that support athletic and artistic activities. Dance, music, and martial arts classes are held after school. Vietnam's larger cities have amusement parks, and several water parks have recently opened in and around Ho Chi Minh City. Youth centers organize entertainment, such as magic shows, plays, and water puppet performances, for local children.

Vietnamese girls and boys have simpler kinds of fun, too, such as riding bicycles, playing card games, and jumping rope. Extra-long jump ropes are made by weaving rubber bands together. One popular children's game is *da cau* (dah cow). The object of the game is to kick a shuttlecock over a net or keep it in the air without letting it touch the ground. The shuttlecock consists of several small, round disks stacked on top of one another, with feathers attached to the top disk. Vietnamese children also enjoy reading. Vendors gather outside schools to sell magazines and comic books. Swimming is another favorite pastime. Children in cities go to public swimming pools, while children living in rural areas or along the coast swim in rivers or the sea.

**TRAVEL**

As Vietnam's economy improves, more Vietnamese families are spending their vacations traveling both in Vietnam and abroad. In 2000, more than eleven million Vietnamese tourists visited well-known attractions in Vietnam, such as the ancient citadel of Hue. The Vietnamese are also beginning to travel overseas in greater numbers. Sixty thousand Vietnamese tourists visited Thailand in 1999. State-owned travel agencies organize trips to destinations such as Singapore, Hong Kong, France, Italy, and Australia.

## Sports

The Vietnamese enjoy and excel at swimming, bowling, soccer, badminton, table tennis (Ping-Pong), volleyball, and martial arts. Golf and tennis were once deemed unacceptable in Vietnam because of their association with Western culture, but these sports are becoming increasingly popular today.

## Soccer

The Vietnamese are passionate soccer fans. Even people who do not actually play the game follow local and international matches. Televised matches of the World Cup draw the highest ratings, beating regular television programs. Regional soccer tournaments held in Hanoi and Ho Chi Minh City attract thousands of enthusiastic fans, and national soccer stars are featured in product advertisements. Some have even appeared in local movie productions. Vietnam hopes to increase its participation in international soccer events. The Fédération Internationale de Football Association (FIFA) and the French Football Federation are supporting Vietnamese soccer by sponsoring the training of promising young players.

*Above:* Nguyen Hong Son of Vietnam tries to score a goal against Cambodia during a match played in Thailand in 2000.

**THE PHU DONG NATIONAL YOUTH SPORTS FESTIVAL**

**The Phu Dong National Youth Sports Festival takes place about once every four years and attracts young athletes from all over Vietnam. The first festival, held in Hanoi in 1983, drew more than seven hundred participants in six events. The Fifth Phu Dong National Youth Sports Festival was one of the ten largest sporting events held in Vietnam in 2000.**

## Vovinam-Viet Vo Dao

The martial arts discipline Vovinam-Viet Vo Dao, or "The Philosophy of Vietnamese Martial Arts," was founded in 1938 by Nguyen Loc. He believed a healthy body and a rational mind are essential to the development of a strong will. After studying and comparing many kinds of martial arts, Nguyen Loc created Vovinam, a martial arts form that develops endurance, speed, and strength. In 1964, philosophical principles were added, and the discipline was renamed Vovinam-Viet Vo Dao. Vovinam-Viet Vo Dao rapidly gained popularity throughout Vietnam and in many other parts of the world.

## Tai Chi, Kung Fu, and Karate

Other popular disciplines in Vietnam include tai chi, an ancient Chinese discipline of meditative exercises, and martial arts such as kung fu and karate. During the Tay Son Rebellion of the 1770s, martial arts became especially popular among the rebels who were trying to unite the country. Today, many Vietnamese people practice kung fu and karate, and Vietnamese athletes win awards at international martial arts championships.

**FROM VIETNAM TO THE REST OF THE WORLD**

In 1980, the Viet Vo Dao World Federation was established. The International Vovinam-Viet Vo Dao Federation was founded in 1990. Today, Vovinam-Viet Vo Dao clubs have sprung up all over Vietnam, and the discipline is studied in countries around the world, including the United States, Canada, France, Italy, and Australia.

*Below:* Early in the morning, many people gather in open spaces to practice the slow movements of tai chi.

# Major Holidays and Festivals

The Vietnamese people traditionally work hard throughout the year. Holidays and festivals therefore provide much-welcome relief from the routine of work. During festive occasions, families and friends get together to enjoy parades, presents, and feasts. Except for national holidays, the dates of many of Vietnam's holidays are determined by the Vietnamese lunar calendar and vary from year to year.

# National Holidays

Several public holidays are held in honor of important milestones in Vietnam's history. The most important of these national holidays is September 2, which is Independence Day in Vietnam. This day celebrates the proclamation of Vietnam's independence by Ho Chi Minh in 1945. Liberation Day falls on April 30 and commemorates the day in 1975 that the communist forces of North Vietnam reunified the country.

# Wandering Souls Day

The fifteenth day of the seventh lunar month is Wandering Souls Day, one of the most important festivals of the year. This day is for remembering the dead. During this time, families worship at home or in temples and pagodas, saying prayers and making offerings of incense and food.

# The Mid-Autumn Festival

The Mid-Autumn Festival is a favorite among children. It is celebrated on the fifteenth day of the eighth lunar month, which usually falls in mid-September. At this time, the harvest moon is at its fullest and appears large and red in the night sky. During the festival, parents buy their children small toys and special cakes, called mooncakes. Families also visit the temple to make offerings of fruits and cooked food. Everyone gathers in the streets to watch exuberant dragon dances. Children are given colorful lanterns in the shapes of dragons, ships, butterflies, and many other objects and animals. The lanterns symbolize light. The Mid-Autumn Festival traditionally represented ancient people's desire for the return of the sun and the long days of summer. After the moon rises, the children parade their lanterns in the streets, beating on drums and singing.

*Above:* **Brightly colored lanterns fill Vietnamese shops as the Mid-Autumn Festival approaches.**

*Opposite:* **Children in Ho Chi Minh City line the streets to watch the parades on Independence Day.**

**TET: THE VIETNAMESE NEW YEAR**

**Tet marks a time of renewal, hope, and goodwill. Welcomed by adults and children alike, the festival is celebrated throughout Vietnam sometime between late January and early February.**
(*A Closer Look, page 70*)

# Food

Chinese, Thai, Indonesian, and French cooking methods have all contributed to the rich and varied dishes served in Vietnamese homes and restaurants. French influences include yogurt, custard tarts, breads, and pastries. The Chinese introduced stir-fry techniques and chopsticks to Vietnam.

Vietnam's cuisine varies from region to region, with three distinctive kinds: southern, central (coastal), and northern. Southern cuisine uses many fresh herbs and the flavors of tropical fruits such as coconuts, pineapples, and papayas. Seafood, including shellfish, squid, and many varieties of fish, characterizes the cuisine of the central coastal region. Northern dishes are similar to Chinese dishes. Dried mushrooms are a common ingredient, and the dishes are often stir-fried.

## Typical Vietnamese Dishes

In Vietnam, most people eat rice three times a day. Rice is served in a large bowl and dished out into smaller bowls. People help themselves to vegetables, meats, and condiments, adding these items to their rice bowls.

*Above:* The durian is a tropical fruit native to Vietnam. The fruit gives off a powerful, exotic fragrance. Its soft, creamy flesh is encased in a thorny shell.

## SWEET TREATS

Vietnamese desserts include fried sweet potatoes and banana fritters; pastries and doughnuts filled with various kinds of bean curd; and sweet soups made from coconut milk, bananas, and other fruits.

*Left:* Roadside vendors in Ho Chi Minh City sell a variety of cooked and uncooked food items.

*Above:* **Vietnamese in Ho Chi Minh City dine at a restaurant.**

*Pho* (fuh), a noodle soup spiced with fresh herbs and served with chicken, pork, or beef, is a standard Vietnamese breakfast. It is sometimes also eaten for lunch or dinner. Some rural villagers eat *xoi* (soy), a dish made of sticky rice mixed with peanuts or mung beans and steamed in a leaf wrapper, for their morning meal.

Many main dishes and snacks are made from pancakes or sheets of rice paper wrapped around various ingredients. *Banh xeo* (bahn say-oh) are pancakes stuffed with prawns, pork, garlic, shallots, and bean sprouts and served with lettuce and a spicy sauce. *Cha gio* (chah yaw), one of the most popular snacks in Vietnam, is a crispy, deep-fried eggroll stuffed with noodles, pork, garlic, shallots, and other ingredients.

*Nuoc mam* (nook mahm), a fermented fish sauce flavored with fresh lime juice, garlic, and chilies, can be used for cooking or as a dipping sauce. In the central region, *nuoc leo* (nook lay-oh), a peanut sauce, and *mam tom* (mahm tohm), a shrimp sauce, are commonly used. Other popular condiments include shrimp paste, lemongrass, ginger, mint, and lime juice.

## TEA AND COFFEE

**Vietnam's highlands support tea and coffee plantations. Tea is served throughout the day. A favorite way of drinking coffee in the country's hot southern regions is to pour it over ice and stir in sweetened condensed milk.**

# A CLOSER LOOK
# AT VIETNAM

A land of great natural beauty, Vietnam is renowned for its wildlife havens. These thriving ecosystems include the majestic Mekong River and mysterious Ha Long Bay. The country's highlands are home to the endangered Javan rhinoceros, the world's rarest large mammal.

Vietnam's geography and landscape have always played an important role in its history and culture. Well-known myths tell of dragons creating landforms such as those found in Ha Long Bay, and the legend of the dragon king Lac Long Quan and the mountain fairy Au Co explains the common origin of all ethnic

*Opposite:* **Tourists explore the Mekong River by boat.**

*Below:* **Vietnamese singers and musicians in traditional dress perform in Hue.**

Vietnamese, as well as the regional differences between northern and southern dwellers. Although the majority of Vietnam's people are ethnic Vietnamese, a fascinating diversity of minority cultures characterizes the country's northern and central highland areas.

Several unique cultural attractions also originated in Vietnam. The ancient art of water puppetry continues to entertain modern audiences in Hanoi and Ho Chi Minh City, and the Cao Dai Great Divine Temple is the center of a religious movement that combines major world beliefs.

# The Ao Dai: A Graceful Outfit

The term *ao dai* (ow yeye) means "long gown." It refers to the traditional dress of the women of Vietnam — a sweeping silk tunic worn over loose, flowing trousers. The tunic has long sleeves, a high neckline, and side slits from the waist to the hem. The trousers reach the soles of the feet and lightly brush the floor. This outfit was designed for comfort in Vietnam's hot, humid weather.

## History

The ao dai first appeared in the eighteenth century, when a Nguyen emperor ordered that all citizens should wear buttoned gowns over trousers. The outfit was adapted from a type of Chinese dress worn by both men and women. The class and social rank of the wearer determined the color of his or her clothing. Yellow cloth was reserved for the emperor, purple for high-ranking court officials, and blue for other court officials. Embroidered designs also indicated rank. For instance, only the emperor could use gold brocade and a five-clawed dragon design.

## The Modern Ao Dai

The ao dai underwent a small revolution in the 1930s, when a Vietnamese fashion designer, Cat Tuong, altered the design. He made the tunic more fitted and moved the buttons from the front to an opening along the shoulder and side seam. Raglan sleeves were added in the 1950s, creating a buttoned seam that stretches diagonally from the collar to the underarm.

For a time after 1975, the ao dai was rarely worn anywhere. Its tailoring was considered an extravagant waste of fabric when many Vietnamese families were extremely poor. People also thought the elegant garment unsuitable for hard work. Today, however, the ao dai is enjoying a revival in Vietnam. In southern Vietnam, the two-piece ao dai is common. In northern Vietnam, the front flap of the tunic sometimes consists of two panels tied together. Men once wore a variation of the ao dai, but with a tunic that was shorter and fuller than the women's tunic. Today, men generally wear the garment only for traditional dance or music performances.

**MANY COLORS**

Ao dai colors and patterns range from solid shades (*above*) and floral designs to flamboyant, hand-painted patterns. Colors often still indicate the wearer's status. For instance, girls commonly wear the ao dai in white, symbolizing innocence (*opposite*). Young unmarried women prefer pastel shades. Strong, dark colors are usually reserved for married women. Bright red is a popular choice among brides.

# The Cao Dai Movement

According to the history of the Cao Dai movement, God revealed Himself in 1919 or 1920 to Vietnamese civil servant Ngo Van Chieu and in the 1920s to a few other men. Under the name of Cao Dai, God ordered the men to establish a new religion to unite existing world beliefs.

The Cao Dai faith was officially founded in 1926. It teaches that all religions have the same origin and worship the same God. Cao Dai principles emphasize the pursuit of oneness with God through the abandonment of worldly desires. Believers devote themselves to the worship of God, to works of service for the community, and to personal purity and purification. Through mediums and channelers at séances, people also contact the spirits of ancestors and famous historical figures to ask for guidance and blessing. Some of these personalities, including Jesus Christ, French heroine Joan of Arc, English playwright William Shakespeare, and Russian dictator Vladimir Lenin, are recognized as patron saints of the faith.

*Below:* **Male Cao Dai priests wear red, blue, or yellow robes. Female priests wear white robes. For the followers of Cao Dai, red is the color of authority and Confucianism; blue, the color of tolerance and Taoism; and yellow, the color of virtue and Buddhism.**

## ORGANIZATION

The basic structure of the Cao Dai movement is similar to that of the Roman Catholic Church. A pope has authority over cardinals, archbishops, bishops, priests, student priests, and disciples. With the exception of the pope, who is divinely appointed, all other positions are determined by election. The positions are open to men as well as women, but only a man can be pope.

# The Cao Dai Great Divine Temple

Located in the province of Tay Ninh, some 62 miles (100 km) from Ho Chi Minh City, the Cao Dai Great Divine Temple is the headquarters of the Cao Dai religion. The temple was built between the 1920s and the 1940s and represents the fusion of Christian, Buddhist, and Islamic architectural styles. Within the temple, pink pillars entwined with green dragons support a high, vaulted ceiling painted blue to represent the heavens. Images of clouds and flying dragons adorn the ceiling.

A typical Cao Dai service at the Great Divine Temple lasts about forty-five minutes and consists of harmonious singing and chanting. After removing their shoes and hats, men enter the temple from the right, and women enter from the left. In the main part of the temple, devotees in white robes worship the Supreme Being, symbolized by the Divine Eye. In the inner sanctuary, at the front of the temple, an eight-sided platform holds a large globe. The all-seeing Divine Eye is painted on this globe. Only high priests may approach the platform to make offerings of candles, incense, flowers, fruit, tea, and wine.

## LASTING POPULARITY

By the 1930s and 1940s, the Cao Dai movement had attracted an estimated 4–5 million followers, including many rural peasants. Under communism, the faith was suppressed from the 1970s to the 1980s. Today, however, the movement has about 2 million followers and is especially popular in the Mekong Delta region. Services are held daily in temples and in private homes.

# The Cu Chi Tunnels

During the Vietnam War, Cu Chi was the site of a large U.S. military base located between important supply areas in Cambodia and Saigon. The Viet Cong created an extraordinary underground network of tunnels beneath the U.S. camp and extending beyond its boundaries. Trapdoors leading to the passages were hidden beneath dense jungle undergrowth.

North Vietnam's communist forces, the Viet Minh, first built the Cu Chi tunnels in 1945 as a defense against the French. South Vietnam's communist forces, the Viet Cong, later expanded the underground network for their campaign against the U.S.-supported South Vietnamese government. Using simple hand tools, the Viet Cong dug the tunnels out of the reddish-brown clay common to the area. This clay was sticky and did not crumble, making it an ideal material for tunneling. The underground network eventually stretched for 124 miles (200 km), from Saigon to the Cambodian border. The tunnels proved crucial to the Viet

*Below:* **A guide demonstrates how Viet Cong forces entered and left the Cu Chi tunnels. U.S. soldiers usually discovered these tunnels only by accident, either by stumbling or falling into them. Such well-concealed hideaways allowed the Viet Cong to stage surprise attacks and avoid capture by the U.S. Army.**

Cong's military success because they also connected Saigon to the supply route that carried weapons, food, and medicine to Viet Cong soldiers in the south.

For years, members of the Viet Cong lived in the tunnels. Although the passages and chambers could hold up to sixteen thousand troops, they usually held between five thousand and seven thousand at a time. Within the tunnels, the Viet Cong built hospitals, kitchens, and sleeping quarters complete with bamboo beds. Storage chambers for food and weapons were carved into the walls. Drinking wells and ventilation tunnels provided water and air. The deepest sections of the tunnels were over 26 feet (8 m) below ground.

U.S. forces were never able to destroy the elaborate tunnel system. Soldiers known as "tunnel rats" were trained to explore the maze of tunnels. The Viet Cong, however, set up false passages and booby-traps to capture or kill intruders. U.S. troops would pump water or gas into the tunnel openings they discovered, but the Viet Cong would seal off these sections to protect the rest of the network. To avoid having their tunnels destroyed by U.S. grenades, the Viet Cong planted major explosives above ground to stop approaching enemies.

*Above, left* and *below:* **The Cu Chi tunnels are now open to visitors who want to explore the underground network. Since the passageways were originally designed for narrow Asian builds, the tunnels have been enlarged to accommodate the broader builds of foreign tourists.**

# The Dragon King and the Mountain Fairy

Folktales and legends have been told in Vietnam since ancient times. Many such stories are explanations of human behavior and the nature of the universe. The legend of the dragon king Lac Long Quan and the fairy Au Co recounts the origin of the Vietnamese race. This myth has been memorized and recited by Vietnamese storytellers for centuries.

   The story begins in the deltas of northern Vietnam, where people lived by fishing and growing rice. King Lai, ruler of the north, had a beautiful fairy daughter named Au Co. One day, a young dragon king named Lac Long Quan arrived in the kingdom and, seeing the radiant Au Co, immediately fell in love with her. Au Co returned Lac Long Quan's devotion, and the two married. Their union produced not a single baby but a golden pouch that contained one hundred eggs. Each egg hatched into a perfectly formed baby boy.

*Below:* The Vietnamese respect the dragon as a symbol of power and majesty. The belief that they are descended from a dragon king has also made the dragon a popular motif in Vietnamese art and architecture. This ceramic detail adorns a gate in the imperial complex at Hue.

*Above:* **Villagers in the province of Binh Dinh celebrate the Lac Long Quan festival with parades and reenactments of the legend. The festival falls in the third month of the lunar calendar (March or April).**

Despite the happiness he shared with Au Co, Lac Long Quan missed his home, the sea. One day, he told his wife that he had to return to the ocean. The fairy took fifty of their children to live with her in the mountains of the north, and the dragon took the other fifty children to the south to live beside the sea. The children living in the mountains grew corn and rice, while those living by the sea fished. During periods of grave danger, the two groups met to confront common foreign enemies.

The Vietnamese believe that the one hundred children of Lac Long Quan and Au Co are the ancestors of Vietnamese kings. This myth explains the cultural differences between the people of the north, associated with China and descended from the serene and intelligent mountain fairy, and the inhabitants of the south, associated with Vietnam and descended from the brave and passionate sea dragon. Despite longstanding cultural and historical divisions between North Vietnam and South Vietnam, the common origin of the Vietnamese people has united them, both politically and culturally, against foreign threats and conquerors for thousands of years.

# Getting Around in Vietnam

Travelers have a wide range of transportation modes to choose from in Vietnam. Boats, from large ferries to tiny rowboats, ply the Mekong River and other waterways. In cities, motorcycles and bicycles zigzag through lines of cars, buses, and trucks. Cyclos, or bicycle rickshaws, also carry locals and tourists.

## On Land

More than six million Vietnamese ride motorcycles or motorized bicycles. Entire industries have evolved in Vietnam to cater to motorcyclists, and highways are lined with stands selling gas, motorcycle parts, and spare tires.

A network of buses serves most areas of Vietnam, including the Mekong Delta, the Central Highlands, and much of northern Vietnam. Large, air-conditioned buses travel from Ho Chi Minh

## TRAVELING BY TRAIN

Between 1899 and 1936, the French built the Transindochinois, a railway connecting Hanoi and Saigon. After 1975, the line was renamed The Reunification Express and remains in service today. Reunification Express trains take passengers through Nha Trang, Da Nang, and Hue on a journey that crosses about 1,056 miles (1,700 km) in thirty-six to forty-four hours.

City along the coast to Hanoi, but buses serving the Mekong Delta tend to be old and badly maintained. Traveling by bus can be slow and unsafe, as Vietnam's roads are constantly undergoing construction work and repair.

Cyclos, or bicycle rickshaws, were first introduced in Hanoi in the 1930s. The cyclo works like a three-wheeled bicycle. The driver pedals from a perch over the back wheel, while passengers ride in a seat supported by the two front wheels. Cyclos, which are bulky and slow, are banned from certain streets in Ho Chi Minh City so they will not hold up traffic. Nevertheless, the vehicle is one of the most common forms of transportation in Vietnam's cities. Sitting in a cyclo is a relaxing way to tour the narrow streets of Hanoi and Ho Chi Minh City. Not reserved exclusively for human passengers, cyclos also transport awkward or heavy items, such as crates of poultry, television sets, and huge potted trees.

## On Water

In a country known for its many rivers and waterways, boats are a practical way to travel. In the Mekong Delta, large, wooden cargo boats carry passengers and goods between villages and cities. Sampans are flat-bottomed rowboats used on rivers. Fishermen sail the South China Sea in junks, or fishing boats with covered decks and tall masts. The junks are anchored some distance from the shore, and people row out to them in small basket boats.

*Above:* **Passengers disembark from a boat at the port of Nha Trang.**

*Opposite:* **Buses in Ho Chi Minh City are so crowded with local commuters that tourists might find the ride very uncomfortable.**

*Below:* **The cyclo is a popular way to get around in Vietnam's cities.**

# Ha Long Bay

Ha Long Bay is located in the Gulf of Tonkin approximately 103 miles (166 km) east of Hanoi. The bay includes more than sixteen hundred islands and islets, one thousand of which have been named. Wind and water have eroded the limestone landscape of the bay, carving out countless hills and rocks, caverns and tunnels, inlets and fjords. These features often resemble animals and have names such as Monkey Island, Turtle Islet, or Crocodile Rock. The nicknames given to other formations, such as the Surprise Grotto and the Grotto of Wonders, reflect the drama and excitement that the bay inspires.

In ancient times, Ha Long Bay was a popular port for traders in Southeast Asia. Rumor has it that the bay was also a haunt for adventurers and pirates. Its many islands and caves were perfect hideouts and headquarters. Today, the Ha Long area is a major center for fishing, agriculture, and shipping. Tourism also supports the local economy.

The thousands of caves, or grottoes, of Ha Long Bay attract millions of visitors every year. The Wooden Stakes Cave, also known as the Cave of Marvels, is one of the most beautiful caves in Ha Long Bay. One of its chambers contains stalactites that look like

*Above:* **Magnificent limestone formations rise from the sea in Ha Long Bay. According to local legend, a family of dragons created the formations, carving out miles (km) of sandy beaches with their thrashing tails.**

a gathering of elves and gnomes. Another cave called the Drum Grotto is named for the faraway drumbeats that seem to be heard when wind rushes through the grotto's stalactites and stalagmites.

## A Protected Area

Among the natural treasures of Ha Long Bay are banks of pink and jade coral, about one thousand species of fish, and numerous kinds of plants and land animals. Archaeologists have also recovered artifacts from local cultures dating back some ten thousand years. These finds have contributed a great deal to current knowledge about the history of Vietnam.

In recognition of the area's natural splendor and cultural and ecological significance, Ha Long Bay was designated a United

*Below:* **The waters of Ha Long Bay sustain a local fishing industry.**

Nations Educational, Scientific, and Cultural Organization (UNESCO) World Heritage Site in 1994. Conservationists in Ha Long Bay are now battling environmental problems such as water pollution from untreated sewage waste. In the 1990s, the World Bank funded a water treatment and habitat protection program for Ha Long Bay. The Vietnamese government aims to develop the local economy by encouraging tourism and improving facilities for businesses. At the same time, economic development needs to proceed cautiously so as not to threaten the rich natural and cultural heritage of the region.

# The Hill Groups of Vietnam

Most of Vietnam's ethnic minorities live in the country's highland areas and make a living from farming, much the same way their ancestors have for centuries. Crops include rice, coffee, and sweet potatoes. Many groups traditionally built thatch-roof huts made of bamboo and raised on stilts. Today, wooden houses are quite common. In very remote hill areas, however, traditional villages still exist.

## The Muong and the Hmong

The Muong inhabit the mountains of north central Vietnam. They number more than 900,000, making them one of the largest ethnic minorities in Vietnam. They are known for their folk literature, poems, and songs. Muong communities rely on farming, fishing, raising livestock, and making handicrafts for a living. They also gather cinnamon and wood for trade with neighboring groups.

The Hmong people live in the mountains of northern Vietnam and parts of China, Laos, and Thailand. Vietnamese Hmong migrated south from China in the nineteenth century and number just over 550,000 in Vietnam today. The Hmong are renowned for their beautiful embroidery work, dances, and folk songs. Hmong subgroups — White, Blue, Black, Red, and Flowered Hmong — are characterized by their distinctive women's outfits. Silver necklaces and clusters of bracelets and earrings enhance the colorful clothing of Hmong women.

Vietnam's highland groups remained largely isolated from the Viet majority for hundreds of years and developed separate cultures. Since 1945, however, communist authorities have changed the lifestyles of many minority groups. Muong farmers, for instance, who used to work on independent farms, now work on community farms and pay a portion of their produce to the state. Faced with shrinking forests and limited land, many other groups have abandoned their traditionally seminomadic or nomadic lifestyles to settle on farms. Anthropologists fear the mountain groups will gradually lose their unique cultural identities as they adopt the lifestyle of the lowlanders.

*Above:* **A woman of the Muong hill group practices stitchery.**

*Opposite:* **Traditionally nomadic farmers, the Hmong have been affected by government regulations on agriculture. The opium poppy, once a valuable cash crop for Hmong groups, is now outlawed in Vietnam. The government has introduced programs to stop poppy cultivation by encouraging farmers to grow substitute crops, such as coffee and tea.**

# Ho Chi Minh

Born Nguyen Sinh Cung to a poor family in 1890, Vietnam's foremost statesman assumed numerous names before settling on *Ho Chi Minh*, which means "He Who Enlightens." He studied in Hue and worked for a time as a schoolmaster in a fishing village bordering the South China Sea.

## Worldwide Travels

In 1911, Ho Chi Minh went to work on a French ship. He traveled to many countries, including the United States and England. In 1917, he settled in Paris, where he became interested in the socialist movement. He began writing articles for radical newspapers and became increasingly involved with communist and leftist groups. He became a charter member of the French Communist Party established in 1920. In 1923, Ho Chi Minh moved to the Soviet Union to study Marxist doctrine; he then traveled to China, where he formed the Vietnamese Revolutionary Youth League. In 1930, he helped to found the Indochinese Communist Party in Hong Kong.

*Below:* **Ho Chi Minh (*in front*) led officials and troops through the North Vietnamese countryside after the French withdrew from Vietnam in the 1950s.**

*Above:* A statue of Ho Chi Minh and a child stands in front of the People's Community Building (formerly the Hotel de Ville) in Ho Chi Minh City.

## Achievements in Vietnam

After thirty years abroad, Ho Chi Minh returned to Vietnam in 1941. He helped found a communist-dominated independence movement called the Viet Minh. Viet Minh forces fought to free Vietnam from Japanese occupation during World War II. In 1945, when the Japanese surrendered, Ho Chi Minh's forces seized control of Hanoi, Vietnam's capital. Ho Chi Minh declared the independence of the Democratic Republic of Vietnam on September 2, 1945. He became president of the new nation.

War broke out in 1946 when the Viet Minh resisted French attempts to reestablish colonial rule in Vietnam. Ho Chi Minh again led his army to battle against foreign occupation. After eight years of fighting, a cease-fire was signed, and French troops withdrew from Vietnam. The country was divided, however, into communist North Vietnam and noncommunist South Vietnam.

When the French left Vietnam, the United States supported the government of South Vietnam against Ho Chi Minh's efforts to unite the two Vietnams. Ho Chi Minh died in 1969, six years before Vietnam finally achieved independence as a united nation.

### A HERO'S LEGACY

Ho Chi Minh was a skilled politician and leader with great charisma. After the end of the Vietnam War in 1975, a mausoleum was built in Hanoi to honor him. Saigon was renamed Ho Chi Minh City in 1976. Today, statues and pictures of the revolutionary hero are displayed throughout Vietnam.

# Ho Chi Minh City

Ho Chi Minh City throbs with the roar of motorcycles, the shudder of old trucks, and the rattle of vendors' pushcarts. For the millions who live here, the nonstop activity is a welcome sign of growing prosperity. This city is filled with both big and small business owners. While large companies set up operations, hair cutters turn stools and mounted mirrors into roadside barber shops, and old women sell bonsai trees from the backs of wooden boxcarts. This enterprising spirit has helped make Ho Chi Minh City a bustling economic and industrial center.

## History

Ho Chi Minh City was founded as a Khmer market town in the fourteenth century and was officially registered as a settlement in 1698. Due to its strategic location on the bank of the Saigon River, the city, then called Saigon, evolved into an important commercial hub. In 1859, French troops invaded Vietnam and captured Saigon

*Below:* **Ho Chi Minh City center is distinguished by prominent land-marks such as the Rex Hotel and the People's Community Building (*right, in the background*), with its French-style façade of arches.**

and several southern provinces. Saigon became the capital of the new French colony. The French built wide, tree-lined boulevards, French-style villas, cathedrals, and public buildings. From 1956 onward, Saigon was the capital of the Republic of Vietnam (South Vietnam). During the Vietnam War, the city was the headquarters of U.S. military operations. In 1975, Saigon fell to North Vietnamese troops. It was officially renamed Ho Chi Minh City in 1976. Under communist rule, Hanoi remained capital of the reunited Vietnam, and Ho Chi Minh City lost its administrative functions.

## A City of Sights

With its sidewalk cafés, numerous museums, and beautiful pagodas and temples, Ho Chi Minh City draws visitors from all over Vietnam and around the world. Among its chief attractions are Reunification Hall, Notre Dame Cathedral, the Historical Museum, and Ben Thanh Market. The Historical Museum houses a stunning collection of artifacts dating as far back as the sixth or seventh century. The ceremonial garments and uniforms of ancient Vietnamese kings and officials are also on display. Ben Thanh Market is one of Ho Chi Minh City's largest and best-known markets. An amazing variety of goods, including cosmetics, clothing, jewelry, flowers, fresh produce, and household items, pack the stalls of the market.

*Above:* **One of the most famous buildings in Ho Chi Minh City, Reunification Hall was built in the 1960s. The building, known then as the Presidential Palace, or Independence Palace, housed the South Vietnamese president until communist forces stormed the palace on April 30, 1975. Reunification Hall is noted for its striking 1960s architecture. Designed by French-trained Vietnamese architect Ngo Viet Thu, the building is shaped to resemble the Chinese character for good fortune. The hall's interior has been preserved as it was found in 1975.**

# Hue: An Ancient Capital

Ancient documents dating back to about 200 B.C. first mention Hue as part of the kingdom of Nam Viet. The city was later conquered by the Cham and then by the Chinese. In the early fourteenth century, Hue passed back into Vietnamese control. In 1802, after several hundred years of civil war, Vietnamese emperor Gia Long united Vietnam and proclaimed Hue the capital of the country. The city remained Vietnam's political capital until 1945, when the communists came to power in northern Vietnam.

## The Royal Capital

At the heart of the city stands Hue's imperial complex, the seat of the Nguyen Dynasty from the mid-sixteenth to the mid-twentieth century. The complex consists of three sections: a city within a city within a city. Under the supervision of Emperor Gia Long, construction began on the outermost citadel, the Capital City, in

*Below:* **The impressive Ngo Mon Gate opens from the Capital City to the Imperial City.**

1805. Tens of thousands of workers labored on the large moated fortress and its watchtowers.

The famous Ngo Mon Gate opens south from the Capital City to the Imperial City. Modeled after the Forbidden City in China, the Imperial City contained courtyards, gardens, temples, towers, and the residences of the royal officials. Just within the city, the Golden Water Bridge, once reserved solely for the emperor's use, leads to the Esplanade of the Great Welcome. Here, civil and military officials dressed in colorful silk robes greeted the emperor by bowing submissively before him. Also in the Imperial City is the Pavilion of Splendor, a temple for the emperors' private prayers. The Nine Dynastic Urns stand near the pavilion. Regarded as national treasures, these bronze works of art are believed to represent nine Nguyen noblemen. Scenes of nature, such as mountains, rivers, plants, and animals, adorn the urns.

The Forbidden Purple City, nestled at the center of the entire imperial complex, was once called the City of Residences. It was designed exclusively for the emperor and his family.

*Above:* The royal library was located within the Forbidden Purple City, along with the royal administrative buildings and the offices of court officials.

## A WORLD HERITAGE SITE

Today, Hue is a popular tourist destination. Its imperial complex was made a World Heritage Site in 1993. The city's ancient tombs, palaces, and other monuments were extensively damaged during the bombing campaigns of the Vietnam War and are currently being restored with aid from UNESCO.

# The Javan Rhinoceros

The Javan rhinoceros, also called the lesser one-horned rhinoceros, was once common throughout Vietnam, Laos, Cambodia, Thailand, Myanmar, and Indonesia. After the Vietnam War, most Western scientists feared that the Javan rhinoceros was extinct in Vietnam. Local Vietnamese, however, continued to report sightings of the animal. In 1989, the carcass of a poached rhinoceros was seen for sale in a marketplace. Further proof that the rhinoceros still lives in the southern jungles of Vietnam came in 1999, when remote-controlled cameras photographed the animal at Cat Tien National Park.

## Dwindling Numbers

During the Vietnam War, defoliants sprayed over Vietnam's forests destroyed much of the rhinoceros's natural environment and its preferred diet of shrubs and small trees. Land mines and hunting posed additional threats to the animal.

The most immediate dangers to the Javan rhinoceros include illegal poaching and the continued destruction of the animal's habitat. Although scientists believe rhinoceros horns have no

*Below:* **The Javan rhinoceros is dusky gray in color. The male of the species possesses a single horn.**

**CRITICALLY ENDANGERED**

Black, white, Indian, and Sumatran rhinoceroses can be seen in North American zoos, but the Javan rhinoceros (*left*) lives only in the wild. After centuries of being hunted, all five species of rhinoceros are currently facing extinction. The Javan rhinoceros, with a population of less than sixty, is currently the species most at risk. According to an examination of hoof prints found in Cat Tien National Park, only an estimated five to eight of these rare animals survive in Vietnam.

medicinal value, the horns remain much in demand as an ingredient in Eastern medicines. Conservationists hope to eliminate the market for rhinoceros horns by encouraging the use of substitute ingredients. To discourage illegal poaching, the Vietnamese government has also set up a rhinoceros reserve patrolled by forest guards.

Today, the Javan rhinoceros lives in only two places in the world — Vietnam and Indonesia. The Vietnamese specimens appear to be significantly smaller than their Indonesian counterparts. This observation leads some zoologists to believe the rhinoceroses of Vietnam represent a unique subspecies of Javan rhinoceros.

Vietnam's Ministry of Forestry, as well as many international conservation groups, such as the World Wide Fund for Nature, the United Nations Food and Agriculture Organization, and the United States Fish and Wildlife Service, acknowledge the urgent need to protect the Javan rhinoceros. Scientists continue to study the habits of this endangered creature in order to strengthen their preservation efforts. Patrol guards are receiving additional training and equipment to help guard the rhinoceros reserve more effectively. Perhaps most importantly, conservationists are enlisting the support of local Vietnamese people by educating them about the Javan rhinoceros and its precious natural habitat.

# Lacquer and Lacquerware

Asian artisans have been creating lacquered objects since ancient times, and Chinese lacquer techniques were introduced in Vietnam centuries ago. According to historical records, a Vietnamese emperor sent an envoy to the Chinese court in the fifteenth century to learn more about the art of lacquerware. Today, Vietnam has a thriving lacquer and lacquerware industry.

## What Is Lacquer?

Lacquer is a resin, or sap, collected mainly from Japanese lacquer trees concentrated in the northern, mountainous province of Vinh Phuc. The sap is fermented, strained, and blended with oil before it is applied to wooden, leather, metal, or porcelain surfaces.

Unlike paint, lacquer is a varnish that must be applied in very thin layers. Before an item can be lacquered, it must be sanded to ensure that the surface is smooth. After each lacquer application,

*Below:* **The creation of fine lacquerware is traditionally a slow, painstaking process. A series of steps and, occasionally, a series of artisans, are required to complete a lacquered object. One craftsperson might make the item that will be lacquered, another might prepare the lacquer, and yet another might complete the final decoration. It can take years to prepare a single piece of fine lacquerware, but lacquered objects can last for generations.**

the lacquered object is dried in a humid, dust-free cabinet for at least twenty-four hours. The dried layer is then polished and another layer of lacquer applied. A single object may have more than one hundred layers of lacquer. Lacquer can be blended with various natural or artificial dyes to create colors.

# Durable Lacquerware

Lacquered items are durable and water resistant; for this reason, lacquer was originally used as a protective coating for boats and barges. Later, lacquer was used to protect and decorate furniture, household items, screens, and musical instruments. In the 1920s, Vietnamese artists learned Western painting techniques, and lacquer techniques that had previously been used for handicrafts were now applied to paintings. Today, lacquer paintings are displayed throughout Vietnam.

# The Mekong River

Measuring some 2,700 miles (4,344 km) in length, the Mekong River flows through southern China, forming part of the Myanmar-Laos and Laos-Thailand borders. It then continues into Cambodia and Vietnam. The river's many nicknames — including Mother of Waters, Turbulent River, Dragon Running River, and Big Water — show the awe and respect people have had for this mighty river through the centuries. In Vietnam, the Mekong is called the River of Nine Dragons, after its nine tributaries.

The Mekong River has sustained an important rice-growing economy for hundreds, perhaps even thousands, of years. The river deposits rich silt on its banks, making the Mekong Delta region fertile for agriculture. During the rainy season, freshwater flows into the delta, nourishing the area's rice crops. Coconuts, sugarcane, pineapples, and various tropical fruits also thrive in the rich soil. Floating markets, consisting of longboats loaded with fruits, vegetables, flowers, and other goods, gather on the river early in the morning. These markets, as well as fishing vessels and passenger boats, contribute to the bustling river traffic in the delta region.

The life-giving Mekong River, however, also poses a serious threat to the homes and farms on its banks. In 2000, flooding was the worst it had been in seventy years, killing close to six hundred people and damaging rice fields, roads, and bridges. Plans are currently underway to install radio-based flood-warning systems and control towers in the river basin.

## The Mekong Ecosystem

Besides its human population, the Mekong Delta is home to an immense variety of animals, such as the Siamese crocodile and the Irrawaddy river dolphin. Some of Vietnam's rarest birds, such as the eastern sarus crane, the world's tallest flying bird, nest in the mangrove wetlands of the Mekong. Pollution, the heavy use of pesticides, and a growing human population threaten the Mekong ecosystem. Organizations such as the World Conservation Union and the United Nations Development Program are working with local governments to protect the natural wildlife of the river basin.

**DELTA OF LIFE**

The Mekong Delta region supports fishing villages (*above*) and waterfront markets (*opposite*).

**CHARTING THE MEKONG**

French naval officers Ernest Doudart de Lagrée and Francis Garnier led an expedition from 1866 to 1868 to explore the Mekong River as a trade route to China. After enduring huge rapids, sandbars, waterfalls, and the death of Doudart de Lagrée from fever, the expedition reached Yunnan Province in China. Although the Mekong was not deemed suitable as a trade route, Vietnam's natural beauty as seen from the river convinced Garnier that the French should expand further into Vietnam in search of trade, raw materials, and natural resources.

# Tet: The Vietnamese New Year

Tet falls in late January or early February and lasts for fifteen days. It marks the coming of spring as well as the new lunar year. For the Vietnamese people, Tet is a time for getting together with friends and family and exchanging gifts and good wishes.

## Making Preparations

As Tet approaches, the streets are filled with busy shoppers carrying bags of candied fruits, decorations, presents, candles, and incense. Families decorate their houses in red and gold and hang woodcut prints of the upcoming year's featured zodiac symbol on the walls. Family members place plum branches and a decorated bamboo pole, symbolizing Tet, in the home for good luck and protection from evil spirits. The pole, stripped of its leaves except for a tuft at the very top, is adorned with bright greeting cards and Chinese symbols denoting prosperity and long life.

## A HEAVENLY JOURNEY

According to Vietnamese legend, just before Tet, the Spirit of the Hearth, Ong Tao, travels to the heavenly palace of the Jade Emperor and reports on matters in each family. People make Ong Tao offerings of food to put him in a cheerful mood as he begins his journey. At midnight on the eve of Tet, the Spirit of the Hearth receives a festive welcome home.

On the eve of Tet, as the sun sets and the new year's first moon appears, special offerings are given to Buddha and deceased family members, who are now invited to join the festivities. As the Spirit of the Hearth is welcomed back to the home, the Tet celebration begins. All family members dress in their finest clothes for the occasion. Children, who are on their best behavior during this time, are rewarded with "lucky money," or cash wrapped in red paper.

The Vietnamese believe that the first days of the new year will determine the fortune of the entire year, so people take care to avoid negative talk and arguments of any kind during Tet. The first visitor to the home on the first day of Tet is also believed to influence the happiness of the family throughout the coming year. If possible, families arrange for their first caller to be a person of wealth and good character. On the first day of Tet, families call on close relatives and friends. Over the next few days, they also visit an extended circle of teachers, acquaintances, and business associates.

*Opposite:* During Tet, people perform dragon dances throughout Vietnam.

# Water Puppetry

Water puppetry, an art form unique to Vietnam, has entertained audiences for almost one thousand years. The craft of water puppetry began in the village ponds and rice fields of the Red River Delta in northern Vietnam. Villagers would gather to watch the performances held in temporary theaters at local ponds. Shows were staged to celebrate the end of rice harvests. Before the show began, farmers would recite prayers for heavy rains and plentiful crops. As early as 1121, water puppet performances were staged for royal audiences in Hanoi.

*Below:* Water puppets are hand carved and stand 2 to 4 feet (0.6 to 1.2 m) high. Each puppet consists of two parts: the body, including a movable head and arms, which is seen above water; and the base, which is usually hidden under water.

For hundreds of years, few people outside the Red River Delta witnessed water puppet performances, and few were trained in the art of water puppetry. Early puppeteers refused to reveal the secrets of their puppetry techniques, passing them down through family generations. Families that knew these secrets would perform together as a troupe. In 1969, the Thang Long Water Puppet Troupe was set up in Hanoi to help preserve the art and train puppeteers. The Thang Long Water Puppet Troupe consists of ten puppeteers and fifteen musicians and technicians. The troupe has traveled throughout Vietnam and around the world, performing water puppet shows in countries such as Japan, France, Australia, Spain, Mexico, and the United States. Today, the Thang Long and other troupes in Hanoi and Ho Chi Minh City give regular performances that captivate locals and visitors.

## A Performance Not to Be Missed!

When a puppet show is ready to begin, the lights dim, and drums, cymbals, and bamboo xylophones begin to pound and crash. Singers and musicians accompany the movements of the puppets. Percussion instruments, such as bamboo bells, gongs, and shells, emphasize the action and maintain the rhythm of the story. The

entire performance is made up of ten to twelve short skits that depict triumphant heroes, dragons and fairies, carefree buffalo herders, and countless other characters. A single performance might involve well over a hundred different puppets.

Modern puppeteers use techniques originally devised by farmers. Hidden behind screens and rattan curtains, they stand thigh-high in water as they control the puppets using bamboo rods, lines, and pulleys. For some skits, the puppeteers operate from boats or rafts. Two or three puppeteers sometimes work together when the action is complicated.

*Above:* **Puppeteers stand thigh-high in water to manipulate the puppets. Apprentice puppeteers typically embark on a six-year training course. They are allowed to perform only after three demanding years of lessons in stagecraft, acting, and singing.**

# RELATIONS WITH NORTH AMERICA

Relations between Vietnam and the United States were limited before the twentieth century. After World War II (1939–1945), the U.S. government's main objective in the countries of Vietnam, Laos, and Cambodia was to stop the spread of communism. Because North Vietnam was strongly influenced by the Soviet and Chinese systems of government, the United States feared that the victory of North Vietnam over South Vietnam would create a strong communist presence in Southeast Asia. From the 1950s onward, the United States began sending military advisers to Vietnam. The U.S. government joined the Vietnam War in 1965, when U.S. president Lyndon B. Johnson ordered the bombing of North Vietnam.

*Opposite:* **Popular North American products, such as Coca-Cola, are easily available throughout Vietnam.**

The Vietnam War dominated twentieth-century relations between the United States and Vietnam. It had a profound effect on the lives of both the Vietnamese and North American people. Many issues arising from the war, such as the status of more than one thousand missing U.S. troops, remain unresolved today.

For almost twenty years after the end of the war in 1975, the United States had no diplomatic relations with Vietnam. In 1994, the U.S. lifted its trade embargo on Vietnam. A year later, the two countries renewed official diplomatic ties. Vietnam and the United States are now working together to promote greater trust and understanding between the two countries.

*Above:* **The Vietnam Veterans Memorial Wall in Washington, D.C., is inscribed with the names of more than fifty-eight thousand men and women who died in or remain missing from the Vietnam War. Dedicated in 1982, the Wall honors all who served in what was the United States' longest war.**

# The Vietnam War

From the mid-1950s until 1975, the United States supported the government of South Vietnam in its struggle against communism. At first, the United States sent advisers to train South Vietnam's military force for defense against the North Vietnamese army. In 1960, communists in South Vietnam formed the Viet Cong, an army dedicated to forcing all foreign armies out of Vietnam. By 1964, North Vietnamese troops were beginning to venture south. Alarmed, the U.S. government changed the status of its Vietnam-based troops in 1965. No longer advisers, they were sent into battle.

U.S. forces were involved in a relentless war against the Viet Cong and their North Vietnamese supporters until 1973. Altogether, more than three million U.S. troops served in Vietnam. Even with superior weapons and helicopter raids, they were unable to defeat the determined Vietnamese communists, who were masters of concealment and ambush, or surprise attack. In 1968, on Tet, the North Vietnamese and Viet Cong launched a surprise attack on thirty-six South Vietnamese cities and towns. The Tet Offensive caused mass destruction throughout South Vietnam. Back in the United States, protests against the war undermined the morale of U.S. troops in Vietnam. The United

*Left:* Helicopter Combat Support Squadron 7 of the U.S. Navy served in Vietnam during the Vietnam War. After the war, members of the unit received a Presidential Unit Citation from U.S. president Richard Nixon for their extraordinary heroism and outstanding performance of duty.

States began a gradual withdrawal from Vietnam, and most troops left by 1973. On April 30, 1975, South Vietnam fell under the control of the North Vietnamese.

## The Legacy of the Vietnam War

The Vietnam War claimed the lives of more than fifty-eight thousand Americans and more than two million North and South Vietnamese people, including civilians. Although the war ended many years ago, its weapons still kill or injure about two thousand people each year. An estimated 3.5 million land mines lie scattered across Vietnam. The U.S. government has provided money to survey the countryside and to purchase mine-removing equipment.

The governments of North America and Vietnam are also cooperating on efforts to locate and identify the remains of North American troops and soldiers listed as "missing-in-action" (MIA). To assist the Vietnamese government in the search for their own missing soldiers, the United States has released documents and assisted in forensic training, or training in the science of identifying or interpreting evidence that could be used in a court of law.

**AGENT ORANGE**

During the Vietnam War, U.S. forces sprayed millions of gallons (liters) of herbicides, including one called Agent Orange, over South Vietnam to kill the dense vegetation that hid enemy soldiers. Bare palm trees (*above*) and tracts of damaged forest were the visible effects of Agent Orange. Although the use of defoliants was stopped in 1971, scientists fear that the residue of Agent Orange is still poisoning thousands of people. The chemical has been linked to birth defects, early cancers, and other medical conditions in human beings. U.S. and Vietnamese authorities are conducting further research on Agent Orange and its effects.

## Current U.S. Relations with Vietnam

In November 2000, U.S. president Bill Clinton became the first U.S. president to visit Hanoi and travel to a unified Vietnam. Several veterans of the Vietnam War accompanied him. His message to both the people of Vietnam and the people of the United States was that Vietnam today should be thought of as a country, not a war.

The United States and Canada are now providing economic assistance to ease Vietnam's transition to a more open economy. The Vietnamese and U.S. governments signed a bilateral trade agreement in 2000. This agreement will open new markets for Vietnam's agricultural and industrial exports and increase U.S. investment in Vietnam.

## Canadian Relations with Vietnam

Canada participated in the Vietnam War by sending troops to Vietnam and selling weapons and equipment to the United States. The North Wall, in Windsor, Ontario, commemorates the contributions of Canadian war veterans and missing troops.

Canadian and Vietnamese leaders have met frequently in recent years. Vietnam's prime minister Phan Van Khai visited

*Above:* U.S. president Bill Clinton (*center*) and Vietnamese president Tran Duc Luong (*left*) review an honor guard during Clinton's arrival ceremony in Hanoi in November 2000.

## U.S. DIPLOMATIC RELATIONS

Ambassador Douglas B. Peterson is the United States' first postwar ambassador to the Socialist Republic of Vietnam. Appointed to Vietnam in 1997, the ambassador continues to work with the Vietnamese government on issues concerning land mines, defoliants, and missing U.S. troops.

Canada in 1994. Canada's prime minister Jean Chretien returned the visit in 1995 and 1997. Since 1996, five Canadian ministers have made a total of six visits to Vietnam.

## U.S. and Canadian Investment in Vietnam

Vietnam's large, well-educated population; raw materials, such as gas and oil; access to the sea; and potential for economic growth make the country appealing to foreign investors. Both the United States and Canada are encouraging Vietnam to continue to open its market, so that a free flow of goods and services can enhance the Southeast Asian nation's growing economy.

The United States is committed to assisting Vietnam's economic development and remains one of the country's export partners. Canada is developing a growing commercial presence in Vietnam. The Canada-Vietnam Business Association was started in 1997 to widen Canadian trade and investment activities. According to the Vietnamese Ministry of Planning and Investment, Canada is the twentieth largest foreign investor in Vietnam. Canadian firms have invested in ventures such as food processing, mining, and other small-scale manufacturing areas.

*Below:* **Billboards along a major highway in Ho Chi Minh City advertise some of the North American businesses that have set up operations in Vietnam.**

# Leaving Vietnam for North America

After the reunification of North Vietnam and South Vietnam, the new government embarked on a policy of severe political repression. Outspoken opponents of the communist government, people who had had ties to the government of South Vietnam, and those who had helped North American forces were imprisoned without trial, either in jail or in reeducation camps. Their homes and property were taken away. Although most of these prisoners were released within a few years, some spent the next ten years in the camps. A wave of Vietnamese emigrants fled their country to avoid imprisonment or persecution. Among them were ethnic minorities who had helped North American forces during the war. This initial wave of refugees to the United States numbered about 130,000.

In the late 1970s and the 1980s, severe poverty and Vietnam's warfare with neighboring countries triggered a second wave of emigration from Vietnam. Many of these refugees escaped in overcrowded boats, becoming known as the Boat People. Survivors of the ordeal landed in Hong Kong, Thailand, Malaysia, and the Philippines, and some then continued their journey to Australia or North America.

*Below:* **The voyage across the South China Sea was extremely dangerous for the Boat People. Drowning, dehydration, and attacks by pirates killed an estimated 30 to 50 percent of the refugees.**

After 1990, the United States received hundreds of thousands of former Vietnamese political prisoners. By 1996, a total of more than 700,000 Vietnamese had arrived in the United States in three waves of immigration.

*Above:* **Little Saigon, in Los Angeles, is filled with Vietnamese restaurants, shops, and supermarkets.**

## Vietnamese in North America

Vietnamese immigrants newly arrived in North America settled in neighborhoods where they could live and work near people who shared their customs and language. As immigrants and their children became increasingly successful, many moved out into the wider community.

The largest Vietnamese community outside of Vietnam is located in California, where more than 200,000 Vietnamese immigrants have settled. Vietnamese-Canadians live mostly in Canada's major cities, including Toronto, Montréal, Vancouver, Calgary, Edmonton, Ottawa, and Winnipeg. Today, Vietnamese-Americans number about 2 million and Vietnamese-Canadians about 136,000. Due to their culture's high regard for hard work and academic achievement, Vietnamese families tend to excel and to prosper financially as they settle into North American life.

# Amerasians

Many North American soldiers who fought in Vietnam during the Vietnam War fathered children by Vietnamese women. When the soldiers returned home after the war, many of these children were left behind. These Amerasians generally faced rejection from local Vietnamese, who looked down on their mixed ancestry. Called "children of the dust of life," many found it difficult to attend school or to secure well-paying jobs. Under the Amerasian Homecoming Act passed in 1987, almost thirty thousand Amerasians have emigrated to the United States.

# Adapting to a New Homeland

Since the Vietnam War, a new generation of Amerasians, Vietnamese-Americans, and Vietnamese-Canadians has emerged. Born and raised in North America, these children of immigrants have adapted more easily than their parents to Western culture. Vietnamese customs, however, remain important to North American families of Vietnamese heritage. Parents want to pass on their traditions and maintain cultural connections with Vietnam. In many cities with large Vietnamese populations,

*Left:* **Many Amerasians in Vietnam hope to emigrate to the United States in search of a brighter future.**

Vietnamese language classes and Vietnamese-language television and radio shows educate younger generations about Vietnamese culture. Vietnamese-Americans and Vietnamese-Canadians also enthusiastically observe traditional celebrations, such as Tet.

## Educational Exchanges

Vietnam and the United States participate in several educational exchanges that benefit both nations. The Fulbright Program was established in 1946 to promote mutual understanding and academic connections between U.S. citizens and other nationalities throughout the world. In Vietnam, the program was initiated in 1992. It enrolls about thirty Vietnamese officials, scholars, and professionals annually in graduate programs at leading U.S. universities.

Massachusetts senator John Kerry is working with other Vietnam veterans to establish a Vietnam Education Foundation. This foundation will support one hundred fellowships every year for Vietnamese students to study in the United States and for U.S. professors of math, science, technology, and medicine to teach in Vietnam.

*Above:* **A children's choir dressed in traditional Vietnamese clothing gets ready to sing the national anthems of Canada and Vietnam during the twenty-fifth anniversary of the end of the Vietnam War observed in Ottawa in April, 2000. Vietnamese culture remains very important to Vietnamese-Canadians.**

# An Ambassador for Peace

One of the most shocking images captured during the Vietnam War was that of a nine-year-old girl screaming and running naked down a road. The girl was Kim Phuc, and her skin was on fire, burned by napalm, a thickening agent mixed with bomb fuel. Kim Phuc's family lived in a village that had been overrun with Viet Cong forces. Under U.S. orders, South Vietnamese planes had bombed the village to destroy Viet Cong troops. The attack, however, killed or injured many innocent people.

After taking the photograph that would earn him the Pulitzer Prize in 1972, U.S. photographer Nick Ut rushed the young girl to the nearest hospital. Kim Phuc's recovery involved seventeen operations and several trips to foreign hospitals for plastic surgery. The photograph taken by Nick Ut appeared on the front pages of newspapers around the world, convincing millions of people of the senselessness of war.

Now a Canadian citizen living in Toronto, Kim Phuc has established the Kim Foundation to help child victims of war. In 1997, she was appointed a Goodwill Ambassador for Peace for UNESCO. In this role, she has traveled to countries such as Bulgaria, New Zealand, Germany, and Ireland to meet with international leaders and promote her message of peace.

*Left:* **Kim Phuc attends a news conference with West German plastic surgeon Rudolf Zellner at his burn clinic in August 1984. Twelve years after suffering napalm burns, she still experienced severe pain from her wounds.**

*Left:* Acclaimed Vietnamese-American filmmaker Tony Bui (*right*) and actor Harvey Keitel (*left*) attended the 1999 Deauville Film Festival in France.

## Movies about Vietnam

The brutality of the Vietnam War inspired a host of movies, including *Platoon* (1986), *Hamburger Hill* (1987), and *Full Metal Jacket* (1987). In *Born on the Fourth of July* (1989), Hollywood celebrity Tom Cruise played a paralyzed Vietnam War veteran consumed by the social and psychological effects of the war.

More recently, Vietnamese-American filmmaker Tony Bui was inspired to write and direct a different kind of film about Vietnam, *Three Seasons* (1999). *Three Seasons* is the first U.S. production filmed entirely in Vietnam. The country's cool, hot, and rainy seasons lend beautiful backdrops to the film's three interwoven plots. In the film, a U.S. Vietnam War veteran searches for the daughter he left behind, a cyclo driver falls in love with one of his passengers, and a young girl who picks flowers at a lotus farm befriends an elderly poet. In 1999, *Three Seasons* won both the Grand Jury Prize and the Audience Award for best dramatic film at the prestigious Sundance Film Festival, held in Utah. Bui's latest film, *Green Dragon* (2001), is set in the first U.S. refugee camp for Vietnamese immigrants, Camp Pendleton, California.

**TONY BUI**

Vietnamese-American filmmaker Toni Bui was born in Saigon in 1973. At the age of two, he moved to California with his family. During visits to Vietnam, he became friends with cyclo drivers, street children, and U.S. war veterans. Their stories inspired him to write and direct *Three Seasons* (1999).

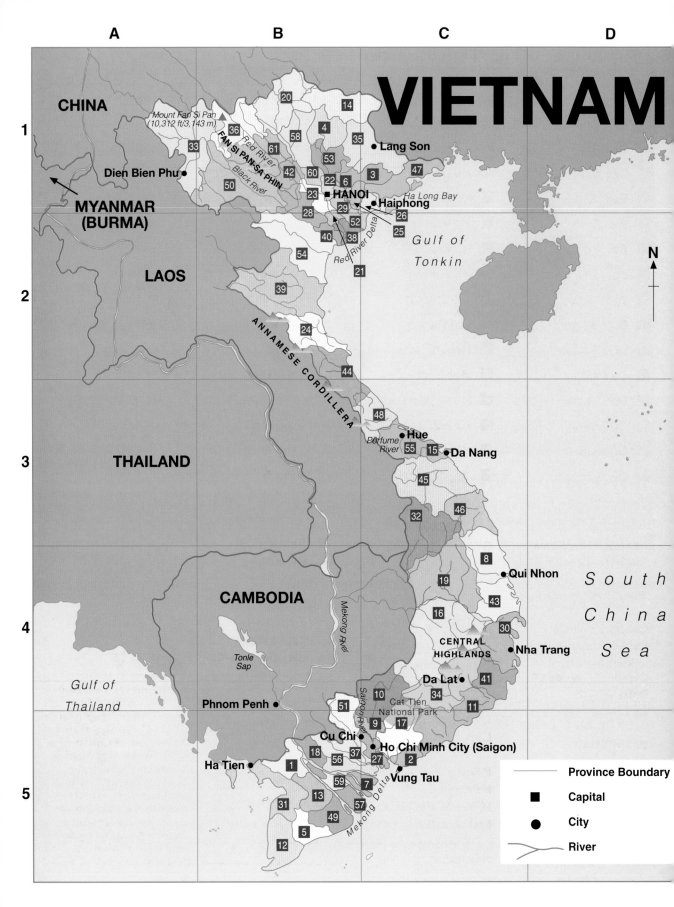

# VIETNAM

CHINA

Mount Fan Si Pan
(10,312 ft/3,143 m)

20

14

36

33

4

35

Dien Bien Phu ●

61

58

Lang Son ●

Red River

FAN SI PAN-SA PHIN

53

42

60

47

50

22  6

3

Black River

23  ■ HANOI

Ha Long Bay

28

29

Haiphong ●

26

MYANMAR
(BURMA)

40  38

52

25

Red River Delta

Gulf of
Tonkin

54

LAOS

39

N

24

ANNAMESE CORDILLERA

44

THAILAND

48

Perfume
River

Hue ●

55  15

Da Nang ●

45

32

46

8

19

Qui Nhon ●

S o u t h

CAMBODIA

16

43

C h i n a

Tonle
Sap

30

CENTRAL
HIGHLANDS

Nha Trang ●

S e a

Mekong River

Da Lat ●  41

Gulf of
Thailand

10

Cat Tien
National Park

34

Phnom Penh ●

51

11

Saigon River

9  17

Cu Chi ●

18

Ha Tien ●

1

56  37

27

2

Ho Chi Minh City (Saigon)

59  7

Vung Tau ●

13

31

57

Mekong Delta

49

12

5

| | Province Boundary |
| ■ | Capital |
| ● | City |
| 〰 | River |

86

# PROVINCES AND *MUNICIPALITIES

1 An Giang

2 Ba Ria-Vung Tau

3 Bac Giang

4 Bac Kan

5 Bac Lieu

6 Bac Ninh

7 Ben Tre

8 Binh Dinh

9 Binh Duong

10 Binh Phuoc

11 Binh Thuan

12 Ca Mau

13 Can Tho

14 Cao Bang

15 * Da Nang

16 Dac Lac

17 Dong Nai

18 Dong Thap

19 Gia Lai

20 Ha Giang

21 Ha Nam

22 * Ha Noi

23 Ha Tay

24 Ha Tinh

25 Hai Duong

26 * Hai Phong

27 * Ho Chi Minh

28 Hoa Binh

29 Hung Yen

30 Khanh Hoa

31 Kien Giang

32 Kon Tum

33 Lai Chau

34 Lam Dong

35 Lang Son

36 Lao Cai

37 Long An

38 Nam Dinh

39 Nghe An

40 Ninh Binh

41 Ninh Thuan

42 Phu Tho

43 Phu Yen

44 Quang Binh

45 Quang Nam

46 Quang Ngai

47 Quang Ninh

48 Quang Tri

49 Soc Trang

50 Son La

51 Tay Ninh

52 Thai Binh

53 Thai Nguyen

54 Thanh Hoa

55 Thua Thien-Hue

56 Tien Giang

57 Tra Vinh

58 Tuyen Quang

59 Vinh Long

60 Vinh Phuc

61 Yen Bai

Annamese Cordillera
  B2–B3

Black River A1–B1

Cambodia A4–C4
Cat Tien National Park
  C4–C5
Central Highlands C4
China A1–D2
Cu Chi B5

Da Lat C4
Da Nang C3
Dien Bien Phu A1

Fan Si Pan-Sa Phin
  (mountain range) B1

Gulf of Thailand A4–A5

Gulf of Tonkin B2–C2

Ha Long Bay C1
Ha Tien B5
Haiphong C1
Hanoi B1
Ho Chi Minh City
  (Saigon) C5
Hue C3

Lang Son C1
Laos A1–C4

Mekong Delta B5–C5
Mekong River A1–C5
Mount Fan Si Pan B1
Myanmar (Burma) A1–A2

Nha Trang C4

Perfume River C3
Phnom Penh
  (Cambodia) B4

Qui Nhon C4

Red River A1–C2
Red River Delta B2–C2

Saigon River B4–C5
South China Sea D2–D5

Thailand A2–B4
Tonle Sap
  (Cambodia) B4

Vung Tau C5

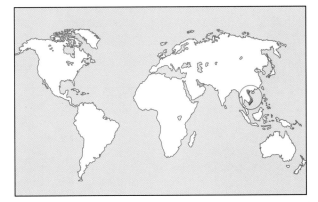

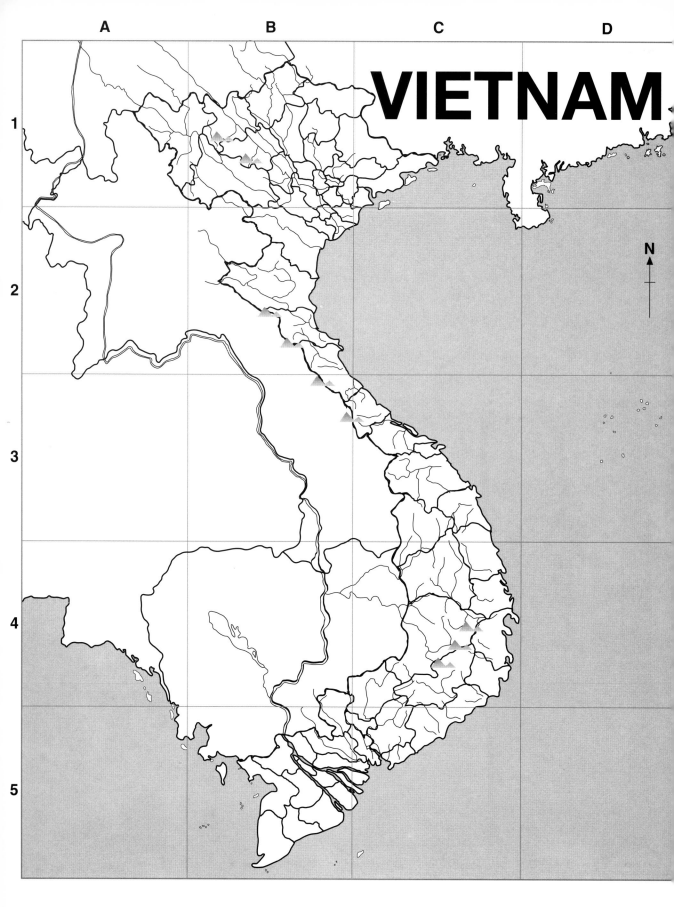

# VIETNAM

A B C D

1
2
3
4
5

N

# How Is Your Geography?

Learning to identify the main geographical areas and points of a country can be challenging. Although it may seem difficult at first to memorize the locations and spellings of major cities or the names of mountain ranges, rivers, deserts, lakes, and other prominent physical features, the end result of this effort can be very rewarding. Places you previously did not know existed will suddenly come to life when referred to in world news, whether in newspapers, television reports, or other books and reference sources. This knowledge will make you feel a bit closer to the rest of the world, with its fascinating variety of cultures and physical geography.

Used in a classroom setting, the instructor can make duplicates of this map using a copy machine. (PLEASE DO NOT WRITE IN THIS BOOK!) Students can then fill in any requested information on their individual map copies. Used one-on-one, the student can also make copies of the map on a copy machine and use them as a study tool. The student can practice identifying place names and geographical features on his or her own.

*Above:* **This little girl is selling food at the seaport of Nha Trang.**

# Vietnam at a Glance

| | |
|---|---|
| **Official Name** | Socialist Republic of Vietnam |
| **Capital** | Hanoi |
| **Official Language** | Vietnamese |
| **Population** | 78,773,873 (2000 estimate) |
| **Land Area** | 127,243 square miles (329,560 square km) |
| **Provinces and \* Municipalities** | An Giang, Ba Ria-Vung Tau, Bac Giang, Bac Kan, Bac Lieu, Bac Ninh, Ben Tre, Binh Dinh, Binh Duong, Binh Phuoc, Binh Thuan, Ca Mau, Can Tho, Cao Bang, *Da Nang, Dac Lac, Dong Nai, Dong Thap, Gia Lai, Ha Giang, Ha Nam, *Ha Noi, Ha Tay, Ha Tinh, Hai Duong, *Hai Phong, *Ho Chi Minh, Hoa Binh, Hung Yen, Khanh Hoa, Kien Giang, Kon Tum, Lai Chau, Lam Dong, Lang Son, Lao Cai, Long An, Nam Dinh, Nghe An, Ninh Binh, Ninh Thuan, Phu Tho, Phu Yen, Quang Binh, Quang Nam, Quang Ngai, Quang Ninh, Quang Tri, Soc Trang, Son La, Tay Ninh, Thai Binh, Thai Nguyen, Thanh Hoa, Thua Thien-Hue, Tien Giang, Tra Vinh, Tuyen Quang, Vinh Long, Vinh Phuc, Yen Bai |
| **Highest Peak** | Mount Fan Si Pan at 10,312 feet (3,143 m) |
| **Major Rivers** | Mekong, Red, Black, Perfume, Saigon |
| **Main Religions** | Buddhism, Taoism, Roman Catholicism, animism, Islam, Protestantism, Cao Dai Movement, Hoa Hao Movement |
| **Major Festivals** | Tet (January/February), Mid-Autumn Festival (September) |
| **National Holidays** | Independence Day (September 2), Liberation Day (April 30) |
| **Exports** | Crude oil, marine products, rice, coffee, rubber, tea, textiles, garments, shoes, handicrafts |
| **Imports** | Machinery and equipment, petroleum products, fertilizer, steel products, raw cotton, grain, cement, motorcycles |
| **Currency** | Vietnamese Dong (VND 14,746 = U.S. $1 as of 2001) |

*Opposite:* **The ruins of a Cham tower stand near Nha Trang.**

# Glossary

## Vietnamese Vocabulary

*ao dai* (ow yeye): a long, flowing tunic worn over long, wide-legged trousers; the traditional dress of Vietnamese women.

*banh chung* (bahn choong): ceremonial cakes made from bean paste, sticky rice, and meat.

*banh xeo* (bahn say-oh): pancakes stuffed with prawns, pork, garlic, shallots, and bean sprouts.

*cai luong* (kye loong): a type of modern opera that originated in Vietnam in the 1920s.

*cha gio* (chah yaw): a crispy, deep-fried eggroll stuffed with noodles and pork.

*cheo* (chay-oh): a type of opera that combines dance, song, mime, and poetry.

*chu nom* (choo nahm): a Vietnamese script used in popular literature before the seventeenth century.

*cyclos* (see-klohs): three-wheeled bicycle taxis.

*da cau* (dah cow): a popular children's game that involves kicking a shuttlecock up in the air.

*mam tom* (mahm tohm): shrimp sauce.

*nuoc leo* (nook lay-oh): peanut sauce.

*nuoc mam* (nook mahm): fermented fish sauce.

*pho* (fuh): noodle soup spiced with fresh herbs and served with chicken, pork, or beef.

*tuong* (toong): classical Vietnamese opera that originated in China.

*xoi* (soy): sticky rice mixed with peanuts or mung beans and steamed in a leaf wrapper.

## English Vocabulary

**animism:** the belief that spirits inhabit both living and nonliving things.

**bilateral:** affecting two countries or sides.

**boulevards:** broad avenues.

**censor:** to examine a text and delete material that is considered harmful.

**chaos:** disorder.

**charisma:** a leadership quality that inspires loyalty; great personal charm.

**charter member:** an original member of a group.

**citadel:** a fortress that commands a city.

**communist:** a person who supports communism, a system of government in which all goods are communally owned.

**compulsory:** required.

**condiments:** substances used to enhance the flavor of food; seasonings.

**defoliants:** chemical sprays applied to plants to cause their leaves to drop off.

**deities:** gods and goddesses.

**delta:** land formed by silt deposits at the mouth of a river.

**dynasty:** a family of rulers.

**embargo:** a government order prohibiting or restricting trade.

**exuberant:** unrestrained and enthusiastic.

**flamboyant:** strikingly elaborate or colorful.

**habitat:** the natural home of a plant or animal.

**hierarchical:** describing a ranked order of people, objects, or values.

**hydroelectric:** relating to the production of electricity by water power.

**imperial:** relating to an empire or emperor.

**impressionist:** relating to or describing the nineteenth-century painting technique of depicting objects by means of strokes of color to resemble reflected light.

**infrastructure:** the system of public works in a country.

**latticework:** a pattern or framework of crossed metal or wood strips.

**leftist:** relating to or describing a political view that favors change in the name of the greater freedom or well-being of the ordinary person.

**levees:** ridges along riverbanks built to control flooding.

**mausoleum:** a large tomb.

**minarets:** tall towers attached to mosques.

**monosyllabic:** consisting of words that have a single unit of spoken language.

**monsoon:** a season of very heavy rainfall.

**muntjac:** a small deer native to Southeast Asia and the East Indies.

**nationalist:** a person who is loyal and devoted to his or her country.

**nomadic:** moving from place to place without a permanent home.

**prestigious:** honored.

**privatization:** the act of selling state-owned businesses to individuals or companies.

**protectorates:** states or territories under the authority of another power.

**radical:** relating to or describing a political view that favors extreme change.

**raglan sleeves:** sleeves with slanted seams extending from the underarm to the neck.

**realist:** relating to or describing the artistic technique of representing objects as they really are.

**regime:** a government in power.

**retaliated:** fought back.

**sandstone:** a rock consisting usually of quartz and some kind of cement.

**sanitary:** relating to health or cleanliness.

**satirical:** describing a literary work that makes fun of human vices and follies.

**séances:** meetings to receive spirit communications.

**seminomadic:** living in temporary homes and practicing seasonal migration.

**silt:** a deposit of river sediment.

**socialist:** a person who supports socialism, a system of government in which all means of production are owned and controlled by the state.

**stalactites:** icicle-shaped mineral deposits hanging from the roof or sides of caves.

**stalagmites:** icicle-shaped mineral deposits that form on cave floors.

**stylized:** having a conventional or artificial form rather than a natural form.

**subordination:** subjection to someone else's authority.

**symbolist:** relating to or describing the artistic technique of using objects to represent ideal or immaterial states.

**tribunals:** courts or forums of justice.

**tributaries:** streams that feed into a river or lake.

**typhoons:** tropical storms with heavy rains.

**zodiac:** a system of symbols representing a particular cycle of time. The Vietnamese zodiac consists of twelve animal symbols that represent a cycle of twelve years.

# More Books to Read

*Children of Vietnam. The World's Children* series. Marybeth Lorbiecki (Carolrhoda Books)

*Stop This War: American Protest of the Conflict in Vietnam. People's History* series.
   Margot Fortunato Galt (Lerner Publications Company)

*Taking Your Camera to Vietnam. Taking Your Camera To* series. Ted Park
   (Raintree Steck-Vaughn)

*Their Names to Live: What the Vietnam Veterans Memorial Means to America.*
   Brent Ashabranner (Twenty First Century Books)

*Two Lands, One Heart: An American Boy's Journey to His Mother's Vietnam.*
   Jeremy Schmidt (Walker & Co)

*Vietnam. Cultures of the World* series. Audrey Seah (Benchmark Books)

*Vietnam. Festivals of the World* series. Susan McKay (Gareth Stevens)

*Vietnam. Major World Nations* series. Wendy M. Cole (Chelsea House)

*Vietnam: The Boat People Search for a Home. Children in Crisis* series. Keith Elliot Greenberg
   (Blackbirch Marketing)

*Water Buffalo Days: Growing Up in Vietnam.* Huynh Quang Nhuong
   (HarperCollins Juvenile Books)

# Videos

*Full Circle with Michael Palin: China, Vietnam and the Philippines.* (PBS Home Video)

*Lonely Planet — Vietnam.* (Lonely Planet)

*Windows to the World: Vietnam.* (Questar)

# Web Sites

www.oxfam.org.uk/coolplanet/kidsweb/world/vietnam/viethome.htm

www.pbs.org/hitchhikingvietnam/

www.vietnamembassy-usa.org/

Due to the dynamic nature of the Internet, some web sites stay current longer than others. To find additional web sites, use a reliable search engine with one or more of the following keywords to help you locate information about Vietnam. Keywords: *ao dai, Ha Long Bay, Hanoi, Ho Chi Minh, Mekong River, Saigon, Tet, water puppets.*

# Index